Paid
Servant

D1383989

Paid
Servant

E. R. BRAITHWAITE

OPEN ROAD

INTEGRATED MEDIA
NEW YORK

Cover design by Mauricio Díaz

ISBN 978-1-4804-5771-3

This edition published in 2014 by Open Road Integrated Media, Inc.
345 Hudson Street
New York, NY 10014
www.openroadmedia.com

Paid
Servant

Chapter
One

As THE UNDERGROUND TRAIN rocked gently on its way I wondered what would happen if I suddenly shouted to my fellow passengers, 'Would any of you like to foster a little boy?' They'd probably think me mad. Even as a joke I wouldn't have the courage to disturb the heavy quiet, broken only by the occasional quick rustle of a newspaper held in such a way that the effect of semi-detachment was continued along the rows of seats. The fact that elbows touched gave no one the right to glance at his neighbour's paper.

The only reading matter I had was the thick file of case-histories in my briefcase—not appropriate reading for the Underground. I was on my way to discuss one of the cases with a London County Council Welfare Officer at her office in the North London Area. A tough case, but, after all, that was why I was appointed to the job, to deal with the tough ones.

After nearly nine years as a schoolmaster in England, I had been seconded from the London County Council's Department of Education to their Department of Child Welfare, to help and advise on the many problems created by the heavy post-war influx of immigrants into Britain from the West Indies, India, Pakistan and other Commonwealth regions. Although I had had no formal training in Welfare work, I had been rather active, for some years, among many immigrant groups in different parts of London, encouraging their efforts to promote self-help schemes of one sort or another. Apparently, some of these extracurricular activities attracted some notice to themselves and it was considered that I had the kind of experience and continuing contact with West Indian and other immigrant groups which fitted me for the job.

Operating from a centrally situated Welfare Office, I was available to all the Area offices for consultation with the Council's Child Welfare Officers who might need help and advice in their dealings with members of the immigrant groups and their children, and to assist in the search for foster or adoptive parents for the increasing number of non-white children who, for a variety of reasons, and either temporarily or permanently, came into the care of the Council—especially the hard-core cases, children who, year after year, remained in the Council's Nurseries or Children's Homes, without any real hope of ever experiencing the warmth of family life. It was hoped that I might have some success with these cases, and though I did not quite agree with the premise on which this hope was based, I was determined to do my best.

Miss Coney was neat; that was the word that came into my mind as we exchanged pleasantries in her office. Everything about her person was neat and orderly; the short, grey-streaked brown hair, trimmed close to her well-shaped head, and the slim, well-proportioned figure in soft tailored tweeds. She was of medium height, her face small-boned, with well-balanced features, and a surprisingly full mouth which would surely have looked sensual with the least touch of lipstick. Her hands were long-fingered, and relaxed, reflecting the confidence she felt in herself, her assured control of whatever the situation would be.

I asked her for some details of the background of Roddy Williams, the young boy whose case I had come to take over from her.

"Ah, yes," she replied. "Rodwell Williams." Her voice was clear and precise. I noticed that she said 'Rodwell'. She took a slim folder from a pile on her desk and went on . . . .

"Not very much on him, I'm afraid. You know about his parents?"

I opened my briefcase and took out the case file on Roddy Williams. Not much there.

Name:	Rodwell Clive Williams
Age:	4½ years
Sex:	Male
Race:	Coloured. Half-Mexican
Father:	Unknown. Thought to have been a United States Service man, probably of Mexican origin.
Mother:	Angela Williams. Present whereabouts unknown. Thought to be a prostitute.
Status:	Available for fostering or adoption.
Remarks:	Abandoned in Holydene

Hospital soon after birth and has since lived
in Franmere Residential Nursery. A hand
some, intelligent, happy child.
Welfare Officer in Charge: Miss L. Coney.
North Central Area.

"It is recorded that his father was unknown, but there's some suggestion that he may have been a Serviceman."

"We don't know for sure," Miss Coney clasped her hands together, "but I think the mother hinted to the hospital almoner that he was an American."

"And the mother?" I said.

"Soon after the child was born she abandoned him in hospital. The hospital almoner got in touch with us and I went round to the address she had given, in Paddington—one of those old buildings now converted to rooming houses.

"She had just got out of bed—at eleven o'clock in the morning—and from the state of the room it was not too difficult to guess what she was up to. She claimed that she had been unwell, and promised to visit the child the following day—but she never turned up.

"I called again at the address in Paddington, but she had moved and we were unable to trace her. Even the police helped us in trying to find her, but without success. So, the child was removed to the Children's Nursery, where he's been ever since. About two weeks ago she turned up here asking to see me, but I was away on leave, didn't get back till yesterday. Perhaps she'll come again."

"Did she leave an address or telephone number?"

"Yes, here it is," she consulted a pad on her desk, "and would you believe it, it's the same place where she lived before."

"Fine," I said, "I think I'll drop around there and have a chat with her."

"That's if she's there. These fly-by-nights are always on the move, you know. I wonder what she wants. Pregnant again, perhaps." Her lip curled in a fleeting expression of distaste.

I asked if there were any further information on the father. "Nobody ever saw him." Miss Coney replied. "The mother told the hospital people that he was an American Serviceman and that's as much as we know. It may well be that she merely picked a man at random from the many she knew."

"But in his file the child is referred to as half-Mexican."

"Well, when you see Rodwell you will understand. I've been in this job for a long time and I can tell. It has to do with his colour and his hair and the shape of his nose and cheekbones. I know about these things."

She smiled confidently, secure in knowing about 'those things'. I thought, 'You'd have a lovely old time in the West Indies or the United States trying to sort them out and label them . . . ' "Has there been any attempt so far to find a foster home for him, or have him adopted?" I asked.

"Oh yes," she replied brightly. "I've been trying for the past three years to have him placed, ever since the Council became his legal guardians. But with coloured children it is not an easy thing. We have to think not only of today, but what will happen when the child grows older. Now and again people have expressed interest, but they've changed their minds when I've explained some of the problems they would have to cope with later on."

"What problems?" I asked.

"Well, you know, there is the problem of placing him in a family where there might be girls. After all, the children won't always be young, and we must think of what could happen in adolescence or later."

I looked at the woman aghast as the penny dropped, setting up its discordant clanging in my mind. Good Lord, under this neat, controlled exterior there lurked all the frightening prejudices which so often made us 'helpers' our own worst enemies, and baulked our best efforts and intentions. Among her equipment was the huge crystal ball of prejudice into which she looked for guidance every time a case involved a coloured person. I could feel the sudden anger rising inside me, making it difficult for me to be reasonable; but I had to be reasonable, and even patient, so that I might learn how it was she approached this case, and with what results. She seemed so nice, so professional.

"I don't quite follow you," I said, purposely not understanding.

"Well, you see, I've had a great many years' experience working among coloured people, and there's not much I don't know about them," she said, calmly.

'Lucky you,' I thought. 'I'm one of them and I know damned little about them.'

"I've had to work among Asians and Africans and West Indians in London and before that in Cardiff, and I know how they feel about things like sex, quite different from the way we English people feel."

As she spoke I wondered where I fitted into this picture. Did the same thing apply to me? Or did my status as a Welfare Officer somehow emasculate me and render me more acceptable?

"In this profession we need to be extremely careful," she went on, her voice cool and easy. "You must forgive me for speaking so frankly to you, Mr Braithwaite, but I think you know what I mean, and considering Roddy's background and everything, we cannot afford to take any chances."

It all came out so smooth and plausible. She must have made up her mind a long time ago about coloured people, and now the ideas had jelled, hardened, ossified. Was there any hope at all of budging her?

I couldn't resist trying. "Well, Miss Coney, being coloured myself, you're making me feel rather awkward in this situation."

"Oh, no, Mr Braithwaite," she exclaimed, her aplomb jarred slightly off centre, "you're different. You're an educated man, and I understand you've lived in England for many years. But . . . ", with a deft twist she had regained her assurance, "thinking of Roddy, I'm sure you will be able to do something for him. You might know some nice coloured family who would be willing to have him so that he can grow up in his natural background. I do hope you understand that I have no prejudice of any kind. Some of my best friends are coloured people, but at the same time one must be realistic about these things, and I'm sure you'll agree that the child would be far better off with people of his own kind."

His own kind. The white part of his origin was not to be considered in this context. I was nettled, but hoping to find some tiny chink in the tight armour of her assurance, I said: "But where do you suppose I shall find foster-parents who have a half-Mexican, half-prostitute background?"

She laughed softly, unperturbed. "Well we must have our little joke, mustn't we?" she replied. "But I'm sure you'll find a place for him. And now I'm afraid I must throw you out, as I've piles and piles of stuff to get through." She stood up and walked around her desk to show me to the door.

Well, that was that. The next step was to see the boy, Rodwell Clive Williams, half-Mexican, half-prostitute. Mix thoroughly for four and a half years. Result should be a cretinous gargoyle at worst, a problem child at best. What was all this talk about a handsome, intelligent, happy child? Maybe that was only the nymph stage and one day, as Miss Coney obliquely predicted, he would surely break through the camouflage and emerge as a fully-fledged sex-motivated problem.

I telephoned the Children's Home where Roddy lived, told the Matron who I was and explained that I would like to visit the boy; she agreed that I could call later that day after the children had had their afternoon nap.

This gave me time to have some lunch before I set off. So I thought I'd travel up to Earls Court and have a snack at the Way-ang, my favourite little coffee bar in Earls Court Road, then make the short run to Wimbledon by Underground.

I had two ham sandwiches and was idling over my second cup of coffee and a cigarette when she came in. She hesitated, half-turned as if to leave, then turned again, a picture of indecision in skin-tight black jeans, thin, flat-heeled shoes and a soiled, tan-coloured duffle coat which hung slackly on her thin frame; long, uneven fair hair half-curtained her face and fell loosely about her shoulders. She took a few steps into the room, looked languidly about her, then walked towards where I sat, somewhat apart from a lively, argumentative group of art students who had apparently discovered the secret of stretching a cup of espresso to last two or more hours. There were several empty seats around the room, and, observing her approach, I hoped she would sit as far from me as possible, but she moved purposefully towards my table, sat opposite me and casually began unbuttoning her duffle coat, the clear, grey, long-lashed eyes, sur-prisingly large in her pale, narrow face. She wore no make-up and without it her small pointed chin and well-shaped mouth looked absurdly childish and immature. The skin of her hands and face was very pale, even transparent looking, and this effect was heightened by the dark, coppery smudges under her eyes.

"Will you buy me a coffee?" Her voice was low and clear, each word spoken separately as if it had been well rehearsed. Somewhat surprised by this direct request I looked into her eyes, met her cool, level glance, and signalled the waitress. I asked for two coffees.

"May I have a cigarette?" Without waiting for reply or gesture from me, she took my cigarette packet from the table and carefully selected one, placed it in her mouth and waited until I got the silent message and hurriedly struck a match for her.

"I hope I'm not making you nervous?" she asked.

"No, of course not, it's a pleasure," I lied.

"Do you mind about the coffee?"

"Oh, no, you're very welcome." I looked around me, wondering whether we were attracting any attention. It must look very much like a rendezvous to any casual observer, and I prefer the women I am with to be, at least, tidy looking. She must have observed my uneasiness.

"I suppose I am embarrassing you," she said. Suddenly she laughed—a sharp, brittle noise which somehow brought no change to her face.

"It'll only be for a little while. I suppose you can stand being embarrassed for a little while?" She rested her elbows on the table, and cupped her face in her hands. She had a trick of letting the smoke slip through her half-open lips in a thick, slow ascending curl, then lazily inhaling it again through her nostrils. Now and then she would tilt her chin upward and blow a thin spear of smoke over my head.

Our coffee arrived and she put two spoonfuls of brown sugar into mine before attending to her own. A charming domestic gesture;

maybe she had a father and brothers and was accustomed to paying them such pleasant little attentions. I noticed her hands, the pale skin revealing a network of blue veins, the fingers long and finely tapered, each index and middle finger deeply stained with nicotine.

"What's your name?"

I looked up. Her eyes were fixed on me. They were clear and clean to their very depths. Whatever had produced the general untidiness had not reached her eyes. Not yet. "Braithwaite, Ricky Braithwaite."

She swung her eyes over me in deliberate, comprehensive summary.

"That's funny. That's really funny. All the Negroes I meet, at school or college, and things, have such ordinary names, such damned ordinary everyday names like Smith and Rogers and Palmer. And now Braithwaite. Mine isn't so simple and everyday. I once had a room-mate, true blue English and all that. Her name was Zutski. Don't you think that's funny?"

I didn't think it was funny. Names don't mean a great deal. "What's your name?" I asked.

Her gaze remained cool, level. No answer. "What do you do?" she asked.

I was on the point of telling her, but changed my mind and mentioned what was still my hobby. "I write," I replied.

"What?"

"Bits and pieces, articles, things like that. I've just published my first book."

"Nice. And what are you?" There was a slight pulling of the muscles around her mouth, the involuntary twitchings of humour, denied, rejected.

"I've just told you, I'm a writer."

"I asked you what you do and now I ask you what you are."

There was a hint of mockery in her voice. "Not the same question, you know, or can't you see any difference?"

I caught on, or thought I did. I thought I had her pegged. Another of those beatnik smarties mouthing the nothing, nowhere philosophy. Anything for a laugh without laughter. I'd met them and heard them. I was suddenly bored with her, bored and a bit impatient.

"Okay. I write and I'm a Negro."

"Is that supposed to mean something?" Without taking her eyes off me she crushed the cigarette butt into the ashtray and reached into the packet for another. I made a light for her.

"I can see you're a Negro," she continued. "The colour of your skin neither impresses nor bothers me." Again she did the trick with the smoke. "I don't suppose you understand. Let's try me. The 'do' part—I was a model, for artists. The 'be' part—I am a singer or rather, that was what I wanted to be. The modelling was for a living while I learned how to sing."

It made sense, the way she put it. "What type of singing?" I didn't ask about the modelling. That was not hard to guess, probably posing for struggling young artists at a few shillings a time.

"What type of singing?" She repeated the question softly to herself, "Blues." She let the word hang between us for awhile and then continued, her eyes now veiled by the long lashes. "Blues. That's the only kind of singing that really matters. You should know, you in your black skin. They say it started with you. I wonder why they called it 'Blues'. Blacks might have been better, but maybe Blues is just right. The only real singing there is. I always had a feeling for Blues, deep inside. Can you sing?"

"No," I replied, "But I love Blues."

She drew hungrily at the cigarette, squinting at me through

the soft, lazy whorls. With her free hand she tilted her coffee cup towards her and made a face at the cold frothy dregs.

"More coffee?"

She nodded and I ordered more coffee.

"How long have you been writing?"

"Off and on about eight years. Nothing much until recently."

"The book?"

"Yes."

"What is it, a novel?"

"No. Biography."

"Oh. They wanted me to do something useful, like marrying somebody, I suppose. My parents, I mean. They paid for me at art school, but I'm not bright enough. Anyway, I didn't do much work. Sat around listening to records and things. Wanted to sing, that's all."

"How did it go, the singing?"

"Not good. It felt good inside here," she touched her chest, "but it didn't sound so good when it came out. You know, not like the professionals. I used to go to hear them whenever I could." She sipped her coffee. "My parents and I quarrelled and I left home."

She blew smoke into the silence between us, then I noticed the tears. She let them run freely from the depths of pain and despair within her, but there was no sound of weeping. Then she rested her head gently on the table and pressed her hands over her ears in the loneliest gesture I have ever seen, as if she wanted to shut out the whole frightening world, the cigarette forgotten but still held between index and middle fingers of her right hand, the blue smoke feathering up from it in a wavering formless pattern.

Into my mind came the memory of the Welfare Chief's recent remarks. How would she view this? Should I tell this girl to go to the nearest Welfare Centre? At what point should I limit my involvement with other people? At what time of day was I off duty?

"Can I help?"

"No." There was something remote about her voice. Remote and final. But low and clear in spite of the tears.

Something else was happening around me and looking away from her I realized that the volume of sound in the coffee bar had decreased. The students were whispering together and glancing in our direction. The sales girl behind the counter was busily minding her own business, but I caught her looking at us. My companion sat up, her face a tear-streaked mess. I took the clean handkerchief from my breast pocket and passed it to her. As she casually wiped her face I noticed that the waitress was standing nearby, looking boldly at me, her eyes bright and hostile. Good Lord, I thought, what must they be thinking? I suddenly felt very uncomfortable under all these speculative stares, and tried to avoid their eyes.

"Sorry about this," she said, "it doesn't mean anything, but I just can't seem to stop it. It doesn't even hurt any more, but it just comes." She tried to smile now, a brave, unsuccessful little effort. I felt very helpless and inadequate.

"How did the singing go? Still trying with it?" Anything to get her talking again, to bring the situation as nearly back to normal as possible.

"No, not now. But I tried to improve it. I started taking singing lessons; so I modelled in the day and worked in coffee bars at night to help pay for them. Then the men wanted me to do more than pose, so I chucked it and went home." She blew her nose, folded the handkerchief into a tight roll, and put it in the pocket of her coat; then she took another cigarette from the packet and I lighted a match; but instead of putting the cigarette to her lips, her fingers slowly shredded it, acting apparently independent of her, then carefully separated the fragments of paper from the tobacco.

"I couldn't remain at home. Mummy was all right, but Dad! It was hell. He seemed to loathe the sight of me. He found fault with my clothes, my hair, my friends, everything. I stuck it as long as I could, then Dad and I had a flaming row, about everything and nothing, you know, and he told me to get out. I had no money. Mummy gave me twenty pounds, all she had, I suppose."

The fingers were painstakingly picking up every bit of paper and tobacco and placing it in the ashtray. "I came and found a little room in Chelsea, on my own. If the men wanted something, they'd pay for it. So I advertised this time. As a model, you know what I mean."

She looked at me; I suppose the look was meant to be defiant, but somehow didn't quite make it. The tears had done nothing to impair the beauty of her eyes.

"Aren't you shocked?"

"No, I don't think so." It was true. I wasn't shocked, or surprised or anything, and I had the feeling that she did not really much care how I reacted. I was merely an ear, available for the moment, needed for the moment. It helped her to talk and it just happened to be me.

"I didn't use my right name. The men came, for all kinds of reasons, and they paid. That's all that mattered, they paid. None of it touched me, can you understand that? None of it really touched me. One day I planned to have enough money to do the thing that really was important to me, and I'd walk out on all of it."

"One day someone rang and made an appointment. The voice was vaguely familiar, but I thought it might have been one of the regulars, you know. He did not say much, just asked if I was free at nine o'clock and when I said 'yes' he hung up. He arrived on time. When he rang the bell I opened the door and there he was—my father. We looked at each other, then he turned and ran. Do you know every time I close my eyes I can hear his footsteps rushing down those stairs. He always wore metal tips on his heels. I cannot sleep for hearing them." Her voice was now barely more than a whisper. "I couldn't work after that, not again. I just stayed in my room. That was two months ago."

"I'm awfully sorry," I said, "it must have been dreadful for you." I knew that it sounded trite, but I felt I ought to say something. She looked so frail and weak and alone. I reached across the table to hold her hand in a spontaneous gesture of reassurance and comfort.

With a small, frightened cry she started, jerking her hand away and upsetting the coffee cups. In her eyes was a look very near terror. I felt confused and humiliated, the more so as now everyone in the coffee bar seemed to be staring at us, at me, the eyes cold and disapproving. The waitress hurried up to clean the mess of spilled coffee, glared at me, and turned to the girl, in immediate sympathy with one of her own sex.

"Are you all right, Miss?"

"Oh, yes, I'm fine," she replied, contrite, "sorry to be so clumsy." She now placed both hands in the pockets of her coat, her body drawn backwards as if involuntarily in retreat. Little girl lost. "I'm awfully sorry," she said to me. "I didn't mean to be rude. It has nothing to do with you. It's just that I can't stand to be touched. Please believe me."

The waitress looked at us, picked up the crockery, and expertly ran a damp rag over the table. She looked questioningly at the girl as if expecting further comment, but my companion only favoured her with a faint smile and the waitress, with another short glance of hostility at me, moved off with her rattling burden.

The girl began buttoning up her duffle coat, probably aware, as I was, that the thing with the coffee cup had broken our *rapport*. "Thank you," she said softly, "you've been a tremendous help, really you have. It's been good of you, listening to me like this. I'm all right now."

With this cryptic remark she stood up, carefully replaced her chair and walked away without another word. On her face was that look of resignation I had sometimes seen on the faces of aircrew just before take-off. I watched her walk through the door and past the glazed front window which overlooked the pavement.

I felt alone and exposed to the curious stares of the other customers, but avoided looking at them and began doodling on the back of an old envelope I had taken from my pocket. I had come here to spend a quiet hour before going on to the Children's Home at Wimbledon, and this had happened. Maybe I was becoming welfare prone, or something. There was still about fifteen minutes before I needed to catch my train, so I decided to stay where I was a while longer. I'd give the girl plenty of time to get far enough away so I would not catch up with her in the street. I don't suppose I'd really been of much help to her. I wondered how her father must be feeling these days. What a hell of a thing to happen to both of them. Maybe I could have lent her a pound or two, but I don't suppose she would have accepted it. She didn't seem to be the type. Oh, well, everyone to his own troubles. I hoped she'd pull through somehow.

I signalled the waitress. I wanted to order another coffee, but she came with the bill. Still hostile. I wondered how she saw us, what kind of situation she placed us in. Probably thought the girl was pregnant, or something like that, and I was responsible. I took the bill, paid the cashier and left. There was no sign of her along the short walk to the station. That was fine; I had no wish to see her again.

There was a number of people milling around excitedly at the entrance to the station, across which a temporary barrier of short iron standards and chains had been placed. Against one of the standards was a blackboard with a hastily chalked notice advising travellers to make their journey by bus as the station was temporarily out of service.

The Children's Home had once been the private residence of a very wealthy family, and in its conversion to its present use many of the lovely archways and curving staircases were preserved. The main building was three-storeyed, with several large rooms on each floor; these had been converted into play-rooms, dormitories, sick-rooms, dining-rooms, rest-rooms, etc., with bedrooms for the resident staff. A well-furnished, self-contained small flat on the ground floor was reserved for the matron of the establishment.

She had seen me coming and was waiting for me at the top of the short flight of stone stairs to the rather showily impressive main door. A tall, well-made woman, with a florid, handsome, smiling face; her white hair was cut short around her head and shone with a silvery sparkle; her eyes were pale blue behind rimless spectacles. There was something positive, strong and secure about her, as of a woman who loved her work and those around her.

"Mr Braithwaite, eh?"

"Good afternoon, Matron."

"Sorry we're so far away off the beaten track." Her strong voice betrayed traces of her Scots origin. She led me to her office. "Well now, let's see. You've come about Roddy Williams. I told him he was having a visitor. He's in the play-room now. You can leave your things here."

I liked this. No waiting around.

He was kneeling on the floor of the play-room before an intricately arranged tower of wooden blocks. In his right hand was another block, poised, waiting; on his face was that look of rapt concentration which few persons manage to achieve after childhood. He was sturdy and well-made, his skin a dark bronze, rich and attractive; his hair was short, of a darker brown and wavy. Handsome in every line of him, strong and handsome. A slim sensitive nose, full lips and a square, dimpled chin; dark brown eyes fringed with long lashes.

I looked at the Matron and surprised a look of such tenderness on her face. "Wonderful, isn't he?" she whispered.

Several other tots were playing their several games around the room, mainly individually, learning in this way to think, to plan, to give their attention to the task in hand. There was no attendant in the room with them. They were already learning to live together peacefully. Some of them noticed our entry but did not interrupt their games. I walked over to Rodwell. He looked up, smiled, and went on with his close study of his structure, planning the placing of the next block.

"Hello," I said.

"Hello," he replied.

I retreated, understanding about him. Matron and I left them to their games.

"Well, what do you think of him?" she asked.

"Grand little fellow," I said.

"Think you'll be able to place him?"

"I hope so. Anyway I'll have a jolly good try."

"Coloured family?"

I watched her closely, tense inside. Jesus, I was getting so damned touchy as soon as anybody said 'coloured'! But it was this thing I'd been meeting right and left, this unspoken presupposition that the word 'coloured' suggested something inferior or second best.

"Not necessarily," I replied. "I would just like to find a nice family in which he can be secure and happy."

"Good for you," she said, "that little man would fit into any good family, I'm sure. You must stay and talk with him."

"I'd like to. Matron, what do you think about Roddy's background? I was speaking with Miss Coney earlier today."

"I know Miss Coney," she said tersely, "and I know her views. I also know Roddy. He was brought here when he was only ten weeks old. I've never seen either the mother or the father, but whoever they are they could have done a damned sight worse than produce such a boy."

Good Lord, the woman was literally bristling in her posture of defence. It occurred to me that if I needed it, I'd get every possible help from her. "Has he had any contact with coloured people at any time?" I asked.

"Not much. One of our local Health Visitors is coloured, from Jamaica. She drops in occasionally to chat with me, and always looks into the nursery to say 'Hello' to the children. Roddy knows her. I suppose when the children are taken out to the park they may see coloured people, but I don't think he knows any other one. Why?"

"I'm just thinking of possibilities, Matron. I'm thinking of people I know, some of them coloured, who have at some time or other talked about adopting children. But if Roddy has never known coloured people that rather narrows the field."

"Why?"

I told her about my recent attempts to find foster-parents for coloured twins, two little girls, who had also spent all their lives in a Home. Although they were very dark-skinned, much darker than Roddy, they were terrified of a black face. It had taken me weeks of persuasive tactics before they had finally accepted me. When now and then I had tried introducing them to another coloured person, the result had been disastrous.

"How old were they?" There was deep concern in the Matron's voice.

"Seven years old."

"What happened? Are they still in the Home?"

"No. I found a white family for them, and they've settled in very nicely."

"Good. But sooner or later they've got to learn to live with their own skins. Maybe it's not that they are afraid of black faces so much as they would like their own faces to be white, you know, to be like all the others they see around them. But I don't suppose there would be that trouble with Roddy; he didn't throw any tantrums at the sight of you. Let's look in and see if he'll talk with you now." She walked ahead of me into the nursery.

Roddy had deserted his tower of bricks and was squatting beside a chubby, flaxen-haired little girl who was seriously explaining something to him as she held up some doll's clothing for his inspection. As Matron and I approached they both turned to look at us. I knelt beside them to make conversation easier.

"Hello," I said.

"Are you Roddy's daddy?" the little girl asked.

"No, I'm Roddy's visitor," I replied.

"What's your name?" she insisted.

"My name's Mr Braithwaite," I replied. "What's yours?"

"I'm Natalie, and my visitor is my daddy."

I left it there. Two and two must always make four in their bright, unspoiled world. Roddy squatted there, coolly regarding me out of his large brown eyes. I'd have to take the initiative with him.

"What were you building over there, Roddy?" I asked him.

"He's making a tower and he wants my table to put on top of it," Natalie interposed before Roddy could open his mouth.

"It's not a table, it's a brick," he said firmly.

"It's a table, and after Goldilocks and Sue are dressed they're going to have tea." She casually indicated two dolls lying patiently naked on the floor while she selected clothing for them from a box which served as a dolls' wardrobe.

"She took it from over there," Roddy continued, pointing to the corner where his incomplete tower stood. "I found her table for her but she won't let me have the brick."

He held up a small, red-painted doll's table, but he was watching Natalie, evidently hoping that our presence would somehow swing the situation to his advantage. But she showed no interest in his unarguable logic; the brick had been converted into a table, and as far as she was concerned it now was a table.

I looked up at Matron and she nodded her head to indicate that we withdraw and leave them to settle the matter as best they could. Back in her office she asked, "Not much chance of talking with him right now, is there?"

"No, but I'd like to pop in as often as I can, so that he gets accustomed to me; and meanwhile I'll see if I can get some people I know interested."

"That's fine, and the sooner the better. It will soon be time for him to begin school, and it would be nice if he were away from here before then."

"That little Natalie's quite a person, isn't she?" I said.

"Ah, yes. She's very independent. Her mother died six months ago, and she's here until her father can make other plans for her. He's in the Army and comes to see her quite often. Well," she said, rising, "nice meeting you. Come down any time you like, and good luck."

I was dismissed. This grand woman had work to do and wanted to get on with it. I liked her.

"Goodbye Matron. You'll be hearing from me soon, I hope."

That evening I prepared a list of people, friends and acquaintances, who might either themselves be interested in fostering a small boy or know of other families who would be willing and able to offer Roddy a home. A very short list really, when one pinned it down to people who had the accommodation, wanted a youngster in the house, and could afford to have him. This last was important and very often proved a stumbling block to people who otherwise would prove excellent parents. Unfortunately, those bureaucrats who determine the policies affecting Child Welfare insist that prospective foster-parents exhibit a very high degree of altruism; not only must they be willing and ready to provide the unfortunate child with a home and all the care and affection which usually flows between parent and child in times of health and sickness, but they must also be prepared to accept the major part of whatever financial burden accrues from it; the prospective foster-parent who is indiscreet enough to raise the question of money immediately becomes rather suspect, and is very likely to be treated as if her interest is primarily in some hope of gain, rather than in the child. Because of this I deliberately limited myself to people whose financial circumstances would suffer the least noticeable strain from the addition of one extra for room and board, and found myself with three possibilities.

1. Mr and Mrs Donald Ellesworth, from Barbados. Donald, a dentist, served in the R.A.F. during the war and now practises in East Finchley. His wife, Audrey, is a part-time teacher at a neighbouring Infants' School, not for the money, she says, but merely to have something to do. Both are about forty years old, but have no children; often talked about adopting a child before they're much older. They own their well-furnished home and each drives a car. I'd known Don and Audrey for about twelve years and they seemed to be a very likely bet.

2. Hardwick and Hannah Rosenberg. Writers. Both highly intelligent and in comfortable circumstances. They have a small child, a girl of three, and have expressed the wish to adopt another, a boy, preferably slightly older than their own child.

3. Dennis and Reena Kinsman. A young South African couple with two youngsters, boys. Comfortably off. I'd placed them last on the list because two boys are a handful in any household, but they might provide a lead to someone else.

Meanwhile I'd seize every possible opportunity to visit Roddy and talk with him and get to know him. As Welfare Officer dealing with the case this was desirable, but even beyond that I felt involved and none of the arguments I held with myself about objectivity in any way seemed convincing. Whether I liked it or not he was a coloured boy, and though the word itself was distasteful, it was unavoidable in a community which placed so much importance on pigmentation or lack of it. His 'blackness' was the main difficulty; that, I was sure, mattered more to Miss Coney than the supposed nature of his mother's activities. Many of the youngsters in the Children's Homes have been born to unwed mothers, and that does not necessarily prejudice their chances of adoption or fostering. I wondered whether the fact of the baby's dark skin may have started the whole rumour about his mother. After all, no one knew for certain that she was a prostitute.

Miss Coney had assured me that she entertained no prejudice, but had more or less admitted that her efforts to find Roddy a home had been limited largely by the colour of his skin. That was an attitude I had been encountering among Welfare Officers, many of whom automatically considered a coloured person as a problem. Some of them felt that a special understanding of the lives of West Indians in their native Caribbean was necessary to winning their co-operation in dealing with them. I did not share that view, but rather favoured the idea that any person, irrespective of his racial origin, was likely to respond favourably to courteous, considerate treatment.

I could not deny to myself that the boy and I were considered to be in the same pigmentation group, and that this gave rise to some feeling of identity with him; but I felt sure that in seeking to find him a home I would be in no way limited by his 'blackness'. If I found a coloured family for him, it would be because I was fully convinced of their suitability, and that Roddy liked them and they him. I also felt sure that there must be many white Britons who would be willing to give him a home. In spite of the wide areas of inter-racial disaffection in many parts of Britain, there was a fund of sincere goodwill waiting to be tapped, and I must be neither too timid, nor too prejudiced, to do the tapping.

Next morning before I left home I rang Don Ellesworth to chat with him before he began the day's surgery.

"Ellesworth here, good morning." Very professional and precise as usual.

"Hello, Don, Ricky here."

"Oh, Hi Ricky; how goes it, boy?"

"Middling. How's Audrey?"

"In the pink. Want to chat with her?"

"Not right away, but I'd like to come over and see you both about something."

"Oh? Care to give me a hint?"

"Sure. Are you still interested in increasing your family?"

He laughed, a deep gurgling sound.

"What are you selling, boy, some new kind of elixir? I don't think your B.G. cure-all herbs will succeed where doing what comes naturally has failed."

"No herbs, Don. A little boy. Made to measure."

"How come? This part of your new job?"

"Yes. But how about it? Interested?"

"Could be. Why not come over and let's talk?"

"Sure. How about tonight?"

"Tonight's fine. See you about 7.30."

He had sounded cautious, but Don was always cautious about

committing himself to anything; if they liked the idea it might be an excellent niche for Roddy, and would very probably help to pull Don and Audrey out of the middle-aged sluggishness into which they were gradually settling. Don had come to England to volunteer for aircrew duty in the R.A.F. in 1941, and later served as a Wireless Operator with a bomber crew. After demobilization he had qualified as a dentist and now had a thriving practice. In the R.A.F. he had been a fine cricketer, tall and athletic, but now he had filled out considerably, and looked what he was, well-fed and prosperous.

Audrey, his wife, was, when I first knew her, short and buxom. A qualified teacher, she had come to England to do an extension course in education soon after the end of the war, but met and married Don instead. She had had three separate attempts at raising her own family, but each had ended in miscarriage, and these failures had somewhat dimmed the sparkle and verve which had been so very much a part of her. She was always well-groomed and healthy-looking, but there was now a droop to her mouth even at her gayest, and she was easily prone to periods of irritability and depression. Neither she nor Don mixed much socially, except with a few doctors or dentists, all of them West Indian, preferring to 'keep themselves to themselves'.

I felt sure that after one look at Roddy they'd be ready to eat out of his hand; he'd certainly set that quiet, refined household ablaze, so to speak. They won't be able to resist him, I thought. I had the feeling that this case would soon be settled and everybody happy; maybe Miss Coney was right after all—a coloured family seemed to be the answer.

Just before noon I went downstairs to make an inquiry in one of the ground-floor offices. As I passed the telephone operator's cubicle she called to me, "Someone's been trying to reach you all morning, Mr Braithwaite. A lady."

I retraced my steps and went over to her; she never missed, not once. Sometimes I'd deliberately try to alter my stride, or even walk on tip-toes, but just as I thought I'd made it, that low, clear voice would reach out to me: "Hello, Mr Braithwaite."

Now I rested a shoulder against the side of her booth and watched the way in which her slim, beautifully-kept fingers moved delicately among the criss-cross of cords or manipulated the switch-keys, unerringly controlling the intricate system. Her head, with its mass of brown, wavy hair was tilted slightly to one side, as if attuned to other sounds besides the unending stream of calls. Her face was plain, with no specially distinguishing feature, except her mouth, which seemed always on the edge of laughter.

"Did the caller leave any message, Miss Felden?"

She felt for the narrow ribbon of paper which hung from the little Braille typewriter on a small table beside her; her fingers quickly traversed the impressed surface and she replied: "No, she'll call again." On her face was a half-mischievous smile, as if she thoroughly enjoyed the short demonstration of the closed mystery between her fingers and the strip of paper.

"Okay, I'll be in my office if she calls again. Got held up at Mile End this morning."

"Gosh, that's awful. Never mind, you're here." The sweetness of smiles was always in her voice, and somehow I could never quite become accustomed to her blindness, or the suggestion of help-lessness which the word invoked. Her general air of assurance and independence was so natural that, whenever in conversation with her, I had the feeling that she had just closed her eyes the better to concentrate on some elusive point, or to listen to some faint sound, and that presently she'd open them again, wide.

"See you later."

I went back to my office. About half an hour later the call came through.

"Mr Braithwaite?"

"Yes, Braithwaite speaking."

"Oh, thank Heaven." There was relief in the voice, relief and a certain husky, lilting inflexion which is distinctly characteristic of the speech of persons from the English-speaking Caribbean territories.

"You don't know me, my name is Bentham, Mrs Bentham. I got your name and telephone number from a friend, and I would very much like to see you about a personal matter."

"Certainly, Mrs Bentham. When could you come to the office?"

"Oh, I wouldn't like to see you at your office," she said, "you see it's family matters, and my friend said you'd come to see us at home. Me and my husband."

"I'm sorry, Mrs Bentham, but I have rather a long list of cases to deal with just now, and I couldn't possibly call at your home today."

"I didn't mean for you to come today," she replied quickly, "my husband and I are both at work during the day, but we'd be in after seven this evening. We'll both be in and it's very important."

"I can't promise to see you this evening, Mrs Bentham, as I am already engaged . . . " I began, when she interrupted.

"My friend said you're a West Indian, and we're from the West Indies too, and it's really very important."

"But could you give me some idea what it is about?" I asked, slightly irritated with her for bringing in the 'West Indian' thing like an identity tag. Did she think it necessary to use that kind of pressure? "Maybe if it's a matter of advice . . . "

"I wouldn't like to discuss it over the phone," she remarked.

There was in her voice a hint of disappointment at my seeming failure to respond to her mention of my West Indian nationality.

"It's a family matter and my friend said you would help us. It's very important and we don't know anyone else to ask for advice."

"Couldn't it wait until sometime tomorrow?"

"Tomorrow might be too late," she replied.

This was not the first of such appeals made to me. Many West Indians now knew of my connection with the Welfare Department and assumed that I would be ready to help at any time they might need me. If I claimed to be too busy or tired it was taken as evidence of snootiness or pride or a disinclination to help them.

"May I have your address, Mrs Bentham?" Probably I might be able to work it in somehow after seeing Don and Audrey. Probably. If it was too much out of the way she'd just damned well have to wait until tomorrow. They lived in Stepney, right across London from Finchley, but on the way to my home in Ilford.

"I can drop in for about half an hour, Mrs Bentham, around 9.30 this evening. I'm afraid I cannot make it any earlier."

Damn it! Why did I have to make excuses for myself?

"Oh, good. Thank you, Mr Braithwaite, we'll see you then." She hung up.

So once again it had happened, and in spite of the Area Supervisor's recent observations and thinly veiled warnings, I could not see that I had any other choice. Besides, what I did in my own time was surely my business—or was it?

The previous Thursday the Area Chief had called me to her office.

"Sit down, please. I've been studying your reports," she began without preamble, "and it seems to me that you are doing too much."

On the desk before her was a batch of documents with which I had been dealing, and near them two letters addressed to me, but opened. I looked at the letters, then again at her, feeling the annoyance mushrooming inside me. From as early as I can remember I've been opposed to anyone opening my letters. My mother had taught me that letters were personal things, and that to open and read someone else's letters constituted an invasion of privacy. I still think so.

"First of all," she continued, picking up the letters, "I've just read these letters addressed to you. Our policy here is to open all letters addressed to officers, and with good reason. Very often in the past we found that important communications were sometimes personally addressed to officers, and because an officer may have been ill or on leave, the communication remained unattended for days or even weeks. We cannot afford to have that happen and advise all members of staff against having any private letters sent to them at this office. I'm telling you this so you will understand why these letters have been opened.

"From what I've read in them it seems to me that, apart from your official duties, you are making yourself privately available to people in your capacity of a Welfare Officer. I would like to suggest that anyone who requires that kind of service from you should apply through the official channels, either through this office, or through any of the other area offices with which you liaise. From the files it is evident that you have as much as you can be expected to cope with officially, and if you are allowed to overwork yourself, your usefulness to the Department will be adversely affected."

Her manner was smooth, unhurried, and very reasonable. But I was still smarting from the sight of the opened letters.

"You've been with the Department a good time now and your results are very satisfactory. It is clear that you are able to get close to your people in a way that your colleagues could not do, or shall we say, have not yet been able to do. This is very useful to the Department, and was one of the chief reasons for your appointment. You can only be fully effective if you husband your strength, especially as you do not have a car. So, in future, if you get requests for help of any sort, I must insist that you direct them to be made officially."

I watched her, as each word separately and distinctly stepped out the short distance between us. The flow of words ceased and the mouth was held compressed in a thin, straight line. Into my head popped a ridiculous idea. What would happen if I said, 'Yes, Sir!'?

"I hope, Mr Braithwaite, that I have made the situation quite clear?"

"Not quite," I replied, still feeling the needle of irritation. "I can understand the necessity for opening letters addressed to officers who are either on leave or ill; but to open them when those officers are on duty indicates a lack of trust in them. If the letters in any way relate to their assignments they should be considered both qualified and able to deal with them; and if they happen to be personal they can be of interest to no one but the people to whom they are addressed."

I paused, but she made no comment and so I continued: "I was seconded here from the Department of Education because it was believed that my own experiences in Britain, and my activities among many of the new immigrants, would contribute to a better understanding of the problems presented by the rapid increase of immigrants into Britain. Obviously, in the circumstances I am bound to receive communications from time to time, and I prefer to deal with them myself. If, arising from those communications, I need advice, help or direction, I would gladly seek it from you or anyone else qualified to give it, but I cannot view the opening of my letters as indicative of trust in my abilities or judgement."

Again I paused, but she sat cool, even detached, regarding me from a distance of miles. The irritation was growing inside me.

"I do not agree with your second point about my off-duty hours. That is my own time, and I'm free to use my own time as I see fit. I never encourage people to seek me out when I am off duty, but I made myself available to help others long before I joined this Department, and I could not retreat from that position merely because I'm now called a Welfare Officer. It was because of the things I learned through being available to people in that way that I'm now able to be of use to the Welfare Department."

"That's all very well," she said, "but your people must not be allowed to get the idea that you are on tap to them twenty-four hours a day."

The 'your people' bit got under my skin. I'd been hearing it long before I became a Welfare Officer, but it seemed more meaningless when used by my colleagues whose training and daily work brought them into close contact with persons from many parts of the world. Many of them, in spite of their training, or perhaps because of its limitations, still saw non-white people as a group, readily identified as blacks or coloureds. I am a Negro, and I was expected to understand anything and everything relative to dark-skinned people. Very often one of them would say, "I had a case today, one of your people," and I would discover that the person was either Asian or African, often in language and custom far removed from my own Caribbean background.

"The people who seek me out are both black and white," I answered with some asperity, "and I'm more concerned with my usefulness to them than with identifying colours or labels."

"You've said nothing to disprove my point." She spoke in the same measured tone, but with a flicker of a smile. "You have no formal training in this field, and there is the real danger of using yourself up through over-enthusiasm. Anyway, I would like you to bear in mind the things I have said, and I am sure there will be no need for disagreement."

That was last week, yet here I was again. Whoever Mrs Bentham was, she did not want to go anywhere near the Area Office. Maybe someone, the same friend, had warned her off. I did not share the view that as a black Welfare Officer I was specially useful in dealing with black people. I was not the least bit concerned with being a black Welfare Officer, and it annoyed me whenever some official mention was made of my appointment, stressing the fact that I was a Negro and therefore, by insinuation, specially qualified to understand the problems of Negroes or coloureds. I believed that any person in difficulty needed help, but most of all he needed to be helped to help himself, so that he could be quickly free from the obligations attendant on help received. The colour of the helping hand was quite unimportant, or should be accepted as unimportant.

My colleagues and I were all paid servants, that is, we were all paid to serve those who needed to be helped and if we were willing, ready and able to serve them well, then as superficial a thing as the colour of our skin mattered not at all, or very little to those whom we served. It seemed to me that the only reason why I had had some little success so far was because I very deliberately placed myself in the position of servant, instead of insisting on being the 'officer', the extension of Departmental authority. My own criterion of my usefulness as a servant lay in the speed with which each new 'case' became independent of both myself and the Department, and was able to manage its own affairs. It could come about not through being 'black', but through trying to understand in each case just where the breakdown in personal confidence occurred, and working hard to restore it, and this applied equally to English, African, Asian, West Indian or anyone else with whom I dealt.

I believed then, and still believe, that there was never any special need in Britain for black Welfare Officers, any more than there is a special need for black judges, bank clerks, fishermen or policemen, or doctors. The urgent need is for a re-orientation of welfare workers in terms of the work they do and the people they serve. They must begin by understanding that British society is irrevocably mixed, and they must expect to serve anyone who comes to them, giving the same courteous, patient, helpful service in each case, for the best of possible reasons, because they are paid to do it. They must be taught the essential psychology of service, the better to bear the failures, frustrations and disappointments which must surely come, and they must be taught about gratitude, or the absence of it, especially from people whose confidence they helped to restore, whose consciousness of dignity they helped to re-establish.

I often listened to my colleagues discussing their cases, and it seemed to me that the gulf between the helper and the helped was often too great for communication and co-operation. True, they were all decent, intelligent, sympathetic people, but I felt that they saw themselves as officers, as people in authority, and everything they said or did was somehow coloured by that authority. I wondered if after working with them, I, too, would adopt the same attitudes, and the thought was both sobering and startling.

The feeling of irritation remained with me. I did not mind about seeing the Benthams even at that late hour, but I minded being expected to see them just because they were West Indians, as if that fact gave them some special priority on my services.

On the other hand, the word had got around about the black Welfare Officer, and I suppose it was unavoidable that I would be expected by coloured people to show them every courtesy, consideration and helpfulness. They would be more critical of any lapse on my part than of a similar shortcoming on the part of one of my white colleagues.

So I put myself at Mrs Bentham's service.

Chapter
Two

THE ELLESWORTHS' HOME, A neat, compact-looking, two-storeyed building, was in a pleasant cul-de-sac at the bottom of a tree-lined side-street. Like its neighbours it was fronted by a thick, well-kept privet hedge, interrupted by a black-painted wrought-iron front gate from which a flagstone pathway led through a small garden of flowering shrubs and miniature lawns to the front door.

Everything about these houses and gardens suggested comfort if not wealth. No one in his right mind could suggest that the presence of this Negro couple could make the neighbourhood less residential, presentable or expensive. I wondered if any stranger could pass by and decide, just by looking at the exteriors, which was the Ellesworth home.

They had waited dinner for me, and it was pleasant to be with them in their comfortable, well-appointed home, enjoying the West Indian dishes which Audrey cooked so expertly. At first the conversation was desultory, then gradually it drifted around to my new job and then to the reason for my visit.

"Don says you'd like us to adopt a little boy." Audrey came to the point rather forcibly. She always prided herself on what she called her directness, but I suspected that it was merely a cover-up for her impatience; she never could wait to find out about anything which interested her.

"Wait a moment!" I exclaimed, "don't rush me. I never said I'd like you to adopt him. I merely asked Don if you two were still interested in adopting a child."

"Same thing, isn't it?" she persisted.

"No, not quite. If you're not interested that's the end of the matter, but if you are, then we can talk about it."

"We've about given up hope now of having any of our own, after a few false starts," Don added, "so if we're to have a family at all we'll have to try ready-mades."

This sounded very promising. It seemed that they had discussed the possibilities and were favourably disposed.

"How do you feel about it, Audrey?" I asked. After all, if anything came of it, she would be the one who would bear the brunt.

"I've been trying to give myself a good excuse to quit this part-time teaching job," she replied, smiling. "It would be fun to spring it on them that I have to stay home and look after my small child." Her smooth, round face creased with mischievous pleasure.

"How old is the child?" Don asked.

"Just four and a half," I replied, keeping the brake on my enthusiasm with some difficulty.

"What's he like?"

"A handsome little devil, very sturdy and sound."

"He's coloured, isn't he?" from Audrey.

"Oh, yes!"

"What happened to his parents?"

"Nobody seems to know anything about the father, and the mother abandoned him in hospital soon after birth."

"From which part of the West Indies is she?" Don asked.

"She's not West Indian. She's English."

They exchanged glances, and immediately I could feel the change in their attitude.

"Oh," exclaimed Audrey, "I thought when you said that he was coloured you meant he was one of us."

"Well, he's not white," I replied lamely.

"That makes it a bit difficult, Rick," Don said. "After all, if we're going to adopt a child we would like to have one which at least looked like us. We don't want to have to explain to people about it. Apart from that, I don't mind putting myself out for one of our own people, but I'm not getting involved with any of the others."

There it was again. 'My people'; 'those people'; 'other people'. They'd not seen the boy and were casually prepared to exclude him from their consideration purely because he was not black enough; the mere mention of the English mother had settled the matter. They were not even interested in the father's origin.

"Poor little bugger," I said. "That leaves him high and dry in no-man's-land."

"Sorry, Rick," Don said, "but it would cause too many complications. If it was a Negro child we might consider it, but as it is . . . ."

Very reasonable and fair, and probably right. But, listening to him, I remembered that this was the same Don with whom I had had so many heated arguments years before when I was passing through a very rough time right here in Britain. In those distant times, he was always holding forth on the illogic of prejudice and

the importance of individual responsibility. Whenever I started
on my anti-white hate quest, he was the person who often talked
about the futility of hate, and the need for positive endeavour to
live above it. Especially that time after the Old Bailey thing; he was
the one who . . .

I had been quite unprepared for it. The envelope seemed so ordinary except for the blue colour and the official O.H.M.S. stamp on
it, that I was flabbergasted to discover that it was a summons to
appear for jury service at the Old Bailey within ten days. Me. And
after all the difficulty and heartache I had experienced in trying to
earn a living. Me—on a jury. It seemed too fantastic for words.

I knew how people were selected for jury service, and the
qualifications necessary to selection. I was a householder (quite a
highbrow name to describe my ownership of the tiny two-up and
one-down house which I had bought as an alternative to paying
excessive room rent near where I worked), and that alone was
enough to qualify me; the powers which summoned one neither
knew nor cared about my state of mind.

I had spoken with Don about the summons and my feelings of
resentment. He had patiently talked about the origins of the jury
system, and the bloody price which Englishmen had paid centuries
ago in order to safeguard this cornerstone of freedom; he reminded
me that I had not been summoned to jury service because I was
black, but because I was a man, a citizen, and I should be proud
to shoulder a citizen's responsibility. He further advised me to live
like a man, with dignity and not let the colour of my skin cripple
my spiritual growth or social consciousness. And he told me then
that our shoutings against prejudice and discrimination would be

empty and meaningless until, inside ourselves, we admitted no difference between men, any men, based on the colour of their skins.

I believed him. I believed all he said because we had shared many similar experiences and had so much in common, and I daily discovered further evidence of the truth of his remarks. But even so, when I went to the Old Bailey, and took my place with the other jurors, I slipped up rather badly; for I missed much of the initial part of the hearing, so intent was I on watching the prisoner, counsel, judge and fellow-jurymen to discover if they were taking any special notice of my presence among them. Only when it was patently clear that they were all too busy attending to the business in hand did it finally sink into my head that my business in that place was to follow the case closely so that I might fulfil the responsibility I had been summoned to undertake . . .

Now this same Don, a little older and more comfortably prosperous, was casually talking about not being involved.

"But everyone else considers him a coloured child," I argued. "I suppose that's the same thing as being Negro. As long as there's any hint of non-white admixture the label is black."

"Yes, I know," he answered. "But people who don't know about us and see the child with us will begin to wonder all kinds of things."

"Is that important?" But even as I asked it I realized that it was important. They were nice respectable people and they did not want complications. If they adopted a child, it must seem to be their natural offspring, and no questions asked. I couldn't quarrel with their attitude, but I couldn't help remembering the old Don. Without realizing it we had both gone very separate ways.

Audrey saved the situation from becoming awkward by suggesting that we had a drink, and somehow the conversation became
diverted to more commonplace things, to everyone's relief.

After I left them I could not throw off the feeling of disappointment. Somehow I felt let down, and the feeling persisted although I
could see the reasonableness of their position. After all, why should
they be more generous than anyone else? I realized that I had been
so sure of their agreement that I had taken their refusal rather hard.
I was not in a frame of mind to be very helpful to the Benthams,
but there was nothing I could do about that. They'd just have to
take me as I was.

Randall Street, Stepney, where the Benthams lived, presented
the dreary picture of a long terrace of dilapidated three-storeyed
houses, all of them covered with scabs of dirt and flaking paint,
and sagging visibly as if impatient of the long overdue demolition
gangs. The mixture of twilight and smoky overcast added to the
general gloomy depression and untidiness of broken railings which
no longer secured any privacy, and large lidless dustbins which
squatted beside the littered area-ways, carelessly pregnant among
the overflow of rubbish. No lights showed in any of the houses, but
the heavy air vibrated with the hum of music escaping from imper-
fectly sealed windows and doors. Indoors it must be awfully loud.

This is what English folk often complain about, I thought. They
don't understand it because they haven't ever felt the need of it.
They don't know that loud music can be needful to the lonely and
rejected, an insulation against pressing loneliness, an opiate for
the hours and weeks of nowhere to go and no one to talk to. As I
approached I could identify the rhythms, the haunting pathos of

songs which spring from an urgent need to survive. Frank Sinatra's "Only the Lonely," each note reaching deep into the consciousness to find the wordless, immediate response.

On the steps of No. 58 Randall Street I paused and looked about me. Farther down the street two men, dimly discernible as Negroes, hurried into a building. Maybe only coloured people live in this street, I thought. The blacks move in and the property loses its value, or so the man said. Then the whites move out. Strange how such supposedly devalued property becomes so shockingly expensive whenever the black man tries to rent or purchase. Randall Street, Negro Section, or Negro Quarter. Quarter of what?

A little way down the street I noticed that the Council had begun putting up new blocks of flats. One fine day they'd reach this spot and put the bulldozers and demolishers to these stinking slums and clear away every last rotting brick to make room for clean, new modern buildings. Then these slum-dwellers would get a chance to live at a greater distance from filth and grime. Or would they? Perhaps they'd be bulldozed and cleared off with the rotting bricks, and forced to find some other blighted dead-end in which to hide and proliferate their miseries; some other rotting slum long devalued and condemned, but still expensive to its numerous black occupants. God, what a stinking vicious circle.

There was no bell or knocker on No. 58, so I rapped with the handle of my umbrella on the rusty letterbox on the door; I continued this rat-tat for about five minutes before the door was opened a few inches and a voice inquired, "Who is it?"

I could dimly make out a shape through the narrow aperture.

"I'm calling to see Mr Bentham," I replied.

"All right, come in," and the door opened wide. I entered a narrow, dimly lighted passage which was partly blocked by a slim, blonde woman who held a dressing-gown or wrapper tightly about her as she looked me over; behind her the passage continued towards a flight of stairs leading upwards. There were closed doors on each side of the passage and I guessed she came out of the one before which she was standing, nearest the front door. Music from several sources mixed to become a tuneless insistent pulse. She seemed in no hurry to stand aside and let me pass, so I asked again, "Where will I find the Benthams, please?"

She turned sideways and nodded towards the stairway.

"Up the stairs and first left." Her voice betrayed a strong North Country accent. As I passed she reached behind her and turned the doorknob to let herself backwards into the room from which dance music suddenly blared out. Ah! I thought. So it's not only the black ones who need the magic boxes to drown their loneliness and despair. From the quick glance I had had of her I guessed she was about twenty-three or twenty-four years old. Did her presence here add to the sordidness of the place, or was it a saving grace?

I went up the stairs, which were covered with sticky linoleum. The upper floor was a replica of the lower, the same narrow, dimly lighted passage between the rooms. I knocked on the first left. It was quickly opened into a room shiningly bright after the outer gloom.

"Oh, Mr Braithwaite, come in. We'd begun to wonder if you'd ever get here."

She was large, nearly as tall as myself, with bare arms shiny smooth from elbow to wrist which somehow suggested muscle rather than fat. Her broad, light brown face was attractive and topped by short, curly, black hair. 'Mixed parentage,' I thought, 'probably Negro and Indian.' Her figure looked good in a dark pleated skirt and frilly white silk blouse; on her feet were soft, inverted sheepskin slippers, the sight of which reminded me of my own tired, aching feet.

"Awfully sorry about being so late," I offered to excuse myself, "but some of my other visits didn't go according to plan."

"Never mind, let me take your bag." She took my briefcase and umbrella and showed me to a chair. "Do sit down. This is Mr Bentham." She waved an arm backwards and he came from somewhere behind her, a small, compact, very dark man, who shook my hand with a surprisingly powerful grip. He was quite bald, yet young-looking, tough and athletic. He wore grey flannel slacks and blue sports shirt open at the neck.

"Gladtomeetyou." He ran the words together as if in haste to get the introduction over with, then moved away and looked at his wife as if waiting for his cue.

"Would you like some coffee, or some rum, perhaps? Have you had any dinner? We could find you something if you like, no trouble at all. We weren't sure when you'd arrive so we've already had ours. Shall I fix some coffee or will you have the rum?" All this without pause.

I was not hungry, only anxious that our discussion should be over as quickly as possible.

While both she and her husband busied themselves with the rum and glasses, I took some notice of my surroundings. The room was not large, but it looked and felt comfortable. A double bed with a gaily patterned coverlet took up most of one side; lengthways against the foot of the bed was a new, black perambulator, shiny with chrome fittings; its hood was neatly collapsed, and I could barely see a bit of hair from where I sat; the infant was evidently sound asleep. In the centre of the wall, opposite the bed, was a deep recess which might once have been a fireplace, but was now concealed by curtains of printed plastic material through the folds of which I glimpsed several suitcases neatly stacked, one upon the other. On one side of the recess was a highly polished radiogram, and on the other a television set. Neatly fitted into a corner near the door was a small gas cooker. The rest of the furniture consisted of a large all-purpose table, two straight chairs and the upholstered armchair in which I sat. The floor was covered in shiny linoleum the colour of simulated marble, and projecting from the wall over the table was a white enamelled metal cabinet from which my hosts were removing glasses. Near my chair a cylindrical paraffin heater made faint blurping noises.

Soon the drinks were ready and we toasted each other's health. Mrs Bentham sat opposite me, but her husband stood leaning against the wall near the pram, evidently somewhat ill at ease. The rum was very potent stuff and seemed to be locating every corner of my stomach with its probing, fiery fingers. I looked from Mr Bentham to his wife, hoping that one of them would start the ball rolling.

"It's about the baby here," he suddenly blurted out, pushing himself off the wall and standing with his legs apart, one hand resting on the edge of the pram. There was something rather defiant about him now. "The mother won't have it, so it's got to go into a home."

He seemed about to say more, but controlled himself with an effort and returned to his position leaning against the wall, and looked at his wife. She sat with her hands clasped in her lap, unruffled.

"Why don't you want your baby, Mrs Bentham?" I asked, puzzled by his outburst and her evident calm. Whatever the matter was I wished they'd hurry up and get to the point. If they thought that they could produce children and then calmly ask the authorities to rear them while they enjoyed themselves, free of responsibility, then I had news for them. Nothing doing!

"Oh, it's not my child," she replied, "and he says it's his," this last with a careless flick of her head in his direction.

"I'm afraid I don't understand. Perhaps one of you would like to explain." I was too tired to play ducks and drakes.

He started to speak, but she interrupted: "Okay, I'll tell it, and if you want to know anything more you can ask him." Her voice carried an odd note of amusement, as if she found the situation, whatever it was, rather funny, in contrast to her husband's grim and somewhat determined expression.

"He got in from work before me last night," she began. "When I got here I saw him with the baby and the pram. He said the baby's mother just brought it and left it with him and told him she couldn't look after it and it was up to him. I told him to take the child back to the mother but he wouldn't. He says she has nowhere to keep it. She only came out of the hospital last week and was staying with friends, now she is going back to her relatives somewhere up North until she feels strong enough to work, or so he says. So now it's up to him." She paused and turned to look at him with that same half-mocking expression on her face.

"But why should the woman bring the child to Mr Bentham?" Even as I asked the question it occurred to me that somehow or other he must be involved with the woman. It was not unusual for babies to be abandoned on doorsteps or churches or railway stations. But I had not heard of anyone dumping a new baby on a stranger with the injunction that he 'get on with it'. Once again he was about to reply, but she beat him to it.

"He says he is the father." Something happened to her face as she said this. Her lips were drawn away from her strong white teeth in a snarl of scorn and her voice took on a hoarse, caustic edge. "That's what he says, but I know it's a lie. Everybody knows it's a lie, except him."

"Shut up, woman," he exclaimed, advancing to stand threateningly beside her, his large fists doubled up by his side. The feeling of pleasant comfort had disappeared from the room. I became conscious of the discomfort of the paraffin heater's warmth and fumes, and noticed for the first time that the only window was tightly closed.

"The child is mine," he continued with controlled vehemence, glancing quickly towards the sleeping infant as if concerned lest our voices disturb it into wakefulness. "I don't give a damn what anyone says, I know it's mine." Then turning to me, "I hear that there are places where a child can be looked after. I am willing to pay for it until the mother comes back. All I want from you is to know where I can take it, just for a few months maybe. I can pay."

He now looked at his wife as if daring her to say otherwise. I thought that the situation was getting rather out of hand, and I did not quite grasp it, nor would grasp it if they kept on yelling at each other and at me.

"Please, Mr Bentham," I said, "your wife asked me to come here because she hoped I would be able to either advise or help you both. She did not tell me anything about the problem and I still don't know just what it is. Now I would like to suggest that you sit down and let us start all over again without exciting ourselves, and if there is any way in which I can be of help to you, you may depend on me. But, as you have invited me here, you might as well tell me the whole story, all of it. I could not advise either of you without knowing all the facts, so please, let's discuss this on as friendly a basis as possible."

He looked at me for a moment, then went to sit on the bed beside the pram, his whole attitude still fiercely protective of the sleeping child.

"Well, it's like this," he began, "I came to England two years ago from Jamaica. I'm a bricklayer, learned my trade at home and before coming here had been working for eight years as a journeyman in Trinidad. Marv, there, was with me in Trinidad, but when I decided to come to England she stayed behind in Jamaica until I found a job and somewhere to live over here—then she would join me. I got a job with a building firm, no trouble at all because I know my trade. I got this room and thought I'd fix it up a bit, you know, get in a few things to brighten it up before Marv came over. Didn't go out much, you know. Got a TV and the record-player, and sort of kept myself to myself."

He paused and rubbed a hand over his head. "Janice, that's the baby's mother, used to come around here to her sister. She lives downstairs."

"Is she the blonde young woman who opened the door to me?" I asked.

"That would be her," he replied. "She's the only white woman living downstairs. There's another one on this floor, Mrs Sobers, married to a man from British Guiana." He got up and retrieved his glass from where he had put it on the radiogram and sipped slowly from it.

"You know how it is," he continued, "we got talking, and sometimes she'd come up and watch TV here, or we'd go to the pictures together. Sometimes her sister would come along with us, you see she lives on her own downstairs, her fellow is in the Forces overseas.

"Janice told me when she knew she was pregnant. Well after all, I knew it was me and I couldn't let her down. So I told her I'd see her through her confinement and afterwards support the child. She knew about Marv and that Marv was coming to join me, and I figured I'd tell Marv about it when she got here, but what with one thing and another it slipped my mind."

"Ha!"

The single explosive sound cannoned out of Mrs Bentham, and the infant began to wail. Before the surprised father could move, his wife had rushed over to the pram and was gently rocking it on its springs. Soon the wailing subsided and she calmly resumed her seat. Her husband went to the table and picked up the bottle of rum to replenish my glass, but I declined; he offered some to his wife but she merely placed her hand over her glass, and he replaced the bottle without adding any to his own drink.

"Where is the child's mother now?" I asked.

"She's gone up North, left yesterday," he replied. "I think she said she has some family in Burnley. She promised to write and let me know where she is."

"You'll wait long for that, I can tell you," his wife intervened. "I've been in England now nearly five months, and the first thing I knew about any baby was when I came home last night to find it here. That woman has dumped the child here and that's the last he'll see of her, even her sister says so. Burnley, indeed!" She sniffed very audibly to emphasize her remark.

"I don't care what her sister says," he replied.

"You should care, Mr Man," his wife exclaimed. Where now was the soft musical voice I had admired when I first heard her? Now she was brutally tough, and yet, how about that little incident with the crying child? I was keenly interested now, though still perplexed.

"You should care," she repeated, "being landed with some other man's child. I was asking around today and everybody says how she's been sleeping with every Tom, Dick and Harry she could find. They know her well. I hear she used to hang around those places in Cable Street, and everybody knows what they're like. Clubs! Ha! I've seen better in a pack of cards!"

"You don't know what you're talking about, woman." His tone was slightly conciliatory, as if his confidence was deserting him and he wanted to steer her away from this line of impugning Janice's character. "You've never even been near Cable Street, so what do you know about it?"

"That's where you're wrong, Mr Man," she exclaimed. "I wasted my lunch-hour today to walk through there just to see it, with all those good-for-nothing layabouts jamming up the pavements. God, somebody should set a match to that stinking hole. You're lucky she didn't give you something else besides somebody's bastard."

Her anger was a deep, heavy thing, throbbing inside her, and reflected in the savage look on her face. I wouldn't like to get on the wrong side of this one, I thought. When worked up she could be really mean.

"Even her sister says she's bad. I talked with her on my way in tonight. Even she says the woman's been sleeping with any black man she could find. Why didn't one of them say it was his? Who do you think you are? What are you trying to prove?"

"Oh, shut up!" he said. "You don't know the girl, you've never laid eyes on her, yet you're in a hurry to believe the worst about her. So what's wrong with Cable Street? And what's so wonderful about Randall Street that makes you look down on other people? I know the child is mine, I even know when it happened. I'm not asking you, I'm telling you. I know. It's my child and nothing you can say will change that." Then to me, "Well, Mister, what do you advise me to do?"

Before I could reply she turned to me: "We've been together

for eighteen years; if he's so good at making children why hasn't he made one with me, eh, why?"

Then she leaned towards him, enraged.

"There's nothing wrong with me, so what about all those years? And where do you think you suddenly got all this fire in your guts to start making children all over the place? I been back with you five months, and still nothing. And you open your big mouth to say you give a white woman a child? Don't talk rass, man." And she swung away from him in apparent disgust.

I thought the issue was quite clear. After years of a childless marriage, a little more than casual association had given Mr Bentham the child he had long wanted, and no amount of argument, scorn or abuse would budge him. The child represented something much more than just an offspring; it was proof of his manhood, and if his wife persisted in her attitude, there was every chance of their marriage being wrecked. They seemed such nice people, admirably suited, yet here they were screaming at each other. Maybe the thought that some other woman, and worst of all, a foreign woman, white woman, had provided what she had failed to give him after eighteen years of marriage, was too big a mouthful for her to swallow. What could I say to them that would be helpful? No matter what happened, this man was prepared to support the child and acknowledge it. Whoever this Janice was, her departure did not seem to worry him in the slightest. Nothing about her seemed to worry him, not her reputation, nothing. He said nothing unkind about her, but he did not attempt to defend her in more than a casual way. Evidently she was merely someone who had been useful in fulfilling a certain purpose and now no longer mattered. The child was important, his child. But what about the marriage? Eighteen years of married life should not so easily be swept away. There must be some way of keeping them together. First of all, I must try to make him realize that placing a child into a Home was not like posting a letter, not by a long chalk.

"I must tell you, Mr Bentham," I began, "that before you can get this baby accepted into a Home, every effort will be made to trace its mother, and it may be necessary to have the police take a hand in locating her."

At the mention of the word 'police', they both looked at each other. "Is that necessary?" she asked.

"Yes, it is, if we cannot locate her by any other means. After all, you may have some doubt about who is the father of the child, but there can be no doubt about the mother."

"Oh, no," he said, "I wouldn't want them to do that, you know, searching for her like a criminal or something. But I've got to put the child somewhere, my wife won't have it in the house."

"I never said that," she flared at him, "I never said I wouldn't have it here. After all, it's not the poor thing's fault, so don't you start putting words into my mouth."

"But I thought . . . "

"You thought!" she continued. "You thought you made a child, so you're liable to think anything else, but don't you twist my words, Mr Man."

"I don't quite understand all this," I said, puzzled. "I thought you were objecting to the child altogether, Mrs Bentham. By the way, what is it, a boy or a girl?"

"A girl," she replied, and suddenly her face lost its stern look. "Some women ought to be shot. Fancy walking off and leaving a helpless little thing like that."

As if on cue, the pram shook on its springs, and the coverings became agitated as the infant vigorously thrust its arms and legs about. Mrs Bentham hurried over to the pram and bent solicitously over its occupant, making soft mother noises to it. Her husband stood up, looked over towards me and shrugged his shoulders, still apparently mystified by the eternally illogical behaviour of women, even after eighteen years of marriage.

"Oh, she's wet. Fetch me a napkin from the case, will you, Jim?" she said, without looking up. He went to the cases in the recess, but soon returned empty-handed.

"There's none there." He hurried outside to see if there were any dry ones on the line.

I watched the woman as she attended the infant, cooing to it in that pleasant jabberwocky women through the ages have used on such occasions. She presented so natural a picture of motherhood that I asked: "What do you expect me to do about this, Mrs Bentham?"

She continued her ministrations for a few moments, then straightened up with the damp napkin in her hand. Dropping it on the floor near the pram she folded her arms across her breast and replied: "I don't want you to do anything, really. I only want him to admit that it's not his child. He knows it's not his, and I want him to admit it."

"But he has said quite clearly that he was intimate with the girl. So even if she had other men, the chances are just as much in favour of him being the father as anyone else. Don't you agree?" I asked.

"That sounds fine," she replied, "but I know what I'm talking about. You see . . . " There was the sound of Mr Bentham's approaching footsteps and she stopped speaking. I had the feeling that she was about to make some further disclosure and wished he had not returned so quickly. He entered the room with a pile of damp napkins in his hand.

"They're still wet," he said, "but maybe I can dry them over the heater."

"Do you want to give the child pneumonia?" she asked him, with some trace of annoyance in her voice. "I think that chemist at Aldgate is open all night; maybe you could take the bus and get some there."

"Okay," he replied, and took his coat from among several outer garments hanging from hooks on the door. He seemed eager to be gone, to have a few moments' respite from this unfamiliar and complicated situation. She remained quite still until she heard the bang of the street door behind him, then, with a smile at me, she said:

"Would you get up a moment, please?"

I stood up, and she casually removed the fitted rubber cushion from the chair to disclose several neatly folded napkins which had been sandwiched between the fabric-covered seat platform and the cushion.

"I put them there this morning, keeps them warm that way," she said, and selecting one, she replaced the cushion.

It was now obvious she wanted to tell me something which he was not supposed to hear. She went again to the baby and applied its clean napkin to the accompaniment of cooing noises. Finished, she sat opposite me.

"You know," she said, "he's a good man, but he's stubborn. Somehow he's got this idea into his head that it's his child and he won't let go."

"Now, please, Mrs Bentham," I intervened, "let's be fair about this. I'm not taking sides in this matter, but your husband has been away from you for about two years and he admits to having an affair with the woman. It is just his misfortune that she became pregnant. Nobody can expect you to be pleased about it, but whether the child stays here or not, if the girl says that he is the putative father and he admits it, he will be legally responsible for its maintenance."

"What was that you said?" she inquired. "What do you mean by putative?"

"It means that he is supposed to be the father, or reputed to be the father."

"Oh, I thought it had something to do with 'puta', you know, it's Spanish; would fit this case, don't you think?" The laughter was back in her voice, deep and generous.

'Bright girl,' I thought, 'very bright girl.'

"You don't understand," she continued, "I'm not cross with him for going with a woman. After all, I didn't expect him to be an angel. What man ever is?"

"Then is it because she is a white woman?" I asked.

"Oh no," she replied, somewhat impatiently, "her colour doesn't bother me. She's a woman, isn't she? It's just that you men are always so sure of yourselves, always so damned sure. His child, pah! Sure he wants a child, don't you think I know that. I've been married to him for eighteen years and I know he's been disappointed because we haven't had children. And so am I. Don't you think I want children, too? His child! His child! How about me?" She stood up suddenly and went over to look at the sleeping infant, then sat on the bed beside the pram.

"I know that all these years he's been blaming me for not giving him children. He never said anything, mind you, but I knew. I could see it in the way he never forgets to buy birthday presents for his sisters' children, so I knew he wanted some of his own. I worried about it for a long time. I even thought that he might some day leave me for someone who could give him children. But he's a good man, Jim is.

"When he first left Jamaica to work in Trinidad, I had to stay behind for sixteen months, before I could join him. I was much younger then, and used to go with a crowd of friends, you know, dances and parties and things. Well, one night after a party I slipped up; you know what I mean, and the next thing I knew I was pregnant.—God, I was frightened. If Jim had found out he might have killed me, or left me. I didn't even like the man, specially. Just one of those unlucky things and the first and only time I ever went with another man. Jim had been gone five months when it happened, so I couldn't tell him it was his, you see?

"Nobody ever knew about it except my mother, God rest her soul! I didn't even tell the man. My mother gave me the money and I got rid of it. So you see, I know this isn't Jim's child. My trouble happened after I had been married for years to Jim, and there's nothing wrong with me. Now, do you understand? And he calmly brings a child to me and says, 'this is mine' and expects me to be pleased about it. Suppose it was the other way round and I had come to him with a child, do you think he would have accepted it?"

There was a little piece of illogic there, because she was saying the child could not possibly be his, whereas if she had turned up with a child he would begin by believing it to be hers.

"I think I understand your position, Mrs Bentham; now how can I help you?"

"Oh, I don't suppose you can, really. All I wanted that man to do was admit that it wasn't his child, but I don't suppose he will. That woman will never come back, I know it, so I suppose I'll just have to look after it, that's all."

I had the feeling she had made this decision long before I ever saw them. "But suppose she does come back, what then?" I asked her.

"I'm sure she's not coming back," she replied with emphasis. "Now that it's here, it stays here. Furthermore, we're moving from here, to one of those new towns perhaps, where it will be able to run about and play. We've got a bit of money put by and Jim can always find work in his trade. He's a good man."

They didn't need me here, not really. For a little while I was useful as a listening ear, or perhaps a needful catalyst to help them resolve the main part of their problem, but now they'd get on fine without me. I stood up and she brought me my bag and umbrella.

"I'm sure you both will work this out satisfactorily, Mrs Bentham," I said, "but if there's anything else I can do, well . . . "

"Oh, don't worry about it," she replied. "I've made up my mind. But that Jim Bentham. So he knows how to make children, does he? Well all right. As of tonight that Mr Man has work to do, right here."

And the rich laughter came burbling out of her in sweet musical waves, rolling back upon her to highlight the richness and beauty of her face and figure and the spirit of love and kindness which shone through them.

As I let myself out of the street door, I thought of Jim Bentham, probably on his way back from the chemist, and the task awaiting him. I laughed to myself. I wondered whoever coined the phrase 'a labour of love'.

As I rode home on the bus I wondered how it would have worked out if I had insisted that the Benthams come to my office if they wanted to see me. Would they have come? And if they had, would they have felt free to speak as they did in their own home? Evidently Mrs Bentham had wanted to talk to someone about her reason for maintaining that the child was not really her husband's. Would she have done so in his presence in the rather formal atmosphere of my office? Could I establish the kind of atmosphere in my office conducive to easy, uninhibited and co-operative discussions?

The only way for me to avoid many of these night visits was to begin at source. I must so conduct myself at interviews in my office that the right atmosphere would be created and inevitably the word would get around, because at the office everything began with an interview. That's where I, too, would have to begin. I'd watched the way some interviews had been transacted, and most of them left a great deal to be desired.

In my mind I tried to review the whole sequence of interviewing which I had witnessed on several occasions, and there was very little about any part of it which could be called commendable. Most persons visiting the Area Office needed help of one sort or another, and invariably appeared looking somewhat fearful or anxious. The physical arrangements of the waiting room did nothing to relieve their anxiety. Its shape, colour and furnishings made it a striking example of the complete lack of imagination characteristic of bureaucratic planning. Pale grey walls unrelieved except by two dreary posters illustrating the increase in road deaths; hard wooden forms ranged alongside the walls and painted the same dark, unhappy brown still to be seen in the waiting-rooms of some rural railway stations; the floor was uncovered, smooth, cold concrete. In this unsalubrious atmosphere the clients waited until they were called to one of the several interview rooms.

Each of these was smaller than the waiting-room, and different in that there were no posters, and instead of forms, the furniture consisted of a table and three chairs. One of these chairs, invariably the most comfortable one, was reserved on one side of the desk for the interviewer. In one corner of each interview room was a little group of rather battered toys, probably intended to attract and maintain the interest of children who accompanied their parents. I have no doubt that this last was often successful, for I often observed small children carefully examining those toys, as if anxious to discover what it was that kept the dirty, battered little monstrosities from falling apart.

I have often wondered why it is that although women occupy most of the senior positions in these Welfare offices they have not been sufficiently revolted by the sterile and miserable condition of the interview and waiting-rooms to bring about some worthwhile improvements in them. Granted the rooms are clean, but so are laboratories and operating theatres. Much more is needed at Welfare offices where, from the very beginning, the entire process of helping must be related to the applicant's dignity and assurance. Could it be that there's something about their single-minded pursuit of a career which cannot accommodate the idea of comfort with service? Or are they so bent on being as much like men as is naturally tolerable that they deliberately favour the severe and regimented in official duties? It has been argued that Social Welfare in Britain is part of State machinery. Granted. But there is nothing which suggests that the work is less efficiently done for a little colour here and there. Welfare Offices are intended as the means by which the State can lend a helping hand to the people. The effectiveness of these officials should depend less on how much help they are able to give than on how quickly those helped become once more independent. If the very first contact with the Welfare Office and Officers helps to speed this process of independence, all the better. A bright, cheerful room with comfortable chairs can inject quite a lift into a depressed spirit, and so, even before the interview, the process of rehabilitation will have begun.

However, in the final analysis, a great deal depends on the officers, and upon their first contact with the applicant. Although quite new to the work, I had visited all of the Areas in London and, with a few notable exceptions, the pattern of interviews was very much the same. The applicant would be called or sent to the interview room, and would sit in a chair on the other side of the table opposite the Welfare Officer, who would often have some files or other documents on the table before her, as if to suggest that she was under heavy pressure. The applicant often sat on the edge of the chair, maybe unconsciously getting the message that the officer's time was valuable, and so prepared for early flight. The first step would be according to the book. The officer would produce a pre-set form, number something or other. I remembered one such interview.

"Your name, please?"

"Maria Coates."

"Age?"

"Twenty-seven."

"Married or single?"

Maria Coates would now put her left hand into her coat pocket. It had been resting on her knee in full view of anyone who cared to look.

"Single."

"Address?"

"47 Welleft Street, NW 10."

"Profession?"

Blushes from Maria Coates, as she looked at the fingers of her right hand in the hope of finding some quick answer. No reply.

"Are you presently employed?"

"No, that is, I was working at a factory, Crannock's, but I left when the baby was on the way. As soon as I get him into a home I'll be able to find another job."

One or two more details and then the form would be put aside and the real business would begin. Undoubtedly I was often very much impressed by the combination of kindliness with efficiency, in probing into the circumstances which led the applicant to seek departmental help; but there was every need to probe, to lift each resistant layer of privacy, as that inherent dignity which is the prerogative of all mankind struggled to keep some little corner of itself inviolate. Yes, the interviewers were kindly and considerate in their way, but they made it clear that they had a job of work to do, and the details they sought were necessarily part of that job. So come on now, give. This is no place to be shy and there are others waiting.

"Have you any relatives who might help you?"

"No, I have a brother in Isleworth, but he's married and he can't do anything for me."

"Maybe if we have a talk with him he'd be willing to help. Can I have his name and address?"

"No, he doesn't know about the baby, and I don't want him to know, not yet anyway. He can't help me, he has a family of his own."

"Any near friend who might help you?"

"No."

"What about the baby's father?"

"No."

"But I'm afraid . . . "

"No."

Now the right hand went into her coat pocket and the garment was drawn tight around her, as if to give some protection against the embarrassing questions. The interviewer changed tactics to:

"How's the baby?"

"He's still in hospital. They say there's something the matter with his lungs, some shadow or something, so he's got to stay there until they're sure he's all right."

Aha! Quite a speech. This was safe ground, talking about the baby, but the girl still seemed unrelaxed and watchful.

"What's his name?"

"I told them up at the hospital it's Michael, Michael John Coates."

"Well, Miss Coates, what would you like us to do for you?"

"Put Michael in a Home until I can get a job and look after him myself. Up at the hospital they told me that if everything's okay with him, I'll have to take him home next Friday. But I'm staying with friends in Willesden and they can't have Michael. There's no room. But as soon as I get a job I could find a room and have him with me. You know, put him in a day nursery in the mornings and collect him at night."

"That's all very well, Miss Coates, but it costs a lot to keep a child in a Home, and it would be some time before you could find a job and a room. Surely Michael's father should help you with him? At least, if it is possible to get Michael into a Home, his father should make some contribution to his maintenance."

"No."

There was something grand about her resolution and spirit. She had guts.

"But why?" There was a note of impatience in the officer's voice.

"From the time I told him I was pregnant he never came near me, never even wrote to me or anything, and when I wrote to him he didn't even answer. Now I don't want to have anything more to do with him and I don't want anything from him."

The lips closed as tight as a trap. That's how she felt and there was no use arguing about it. 'Bravo!' I thought.

The officer realized that there was no use pursuing that line, and said:

"Well, Miss Coates, I'll have a word with the Supervisor and we'll see what we can do. We'll get in touch with the hospital to inquire about the baby's illness. Could you call here again in a few days, say next Thursday, then I'll let you know what's been decided."

"Thank you."

End of interview.

That was the pattern, with the officer's position and that of the applicant clearly defined. From what I'd heard, the relationship generally improved as the interviews increased in number, and officer and applicant became accustomed to each other. But that necessarily took time and there weren't enough officers to allow for such waste. It seemed to me that it was quite possible to establish a better working relationship with an applicant from the very beginning. Instead of sitting on the edge of a chair with her legs tucked under in tense unease, she should be relaxed, or as nearly so as her own anxieties and problems would permit, and assured of the officer's help and service. Yes, service. At most interviews I witnessed officialdom but not service. The officer was the kingpin, firmly in the seat of authority. To serve was consciously to reverse the position, and to make the applicant conscious of being served. Everything should be geared to that. I'd really think about it and try to work it out at my own interviews.

Chapter
Three

Early next morning I rang the Rosenbergs. Hannah answered. When I told her about Roddy, she was delighted, and asked me to come round to discuss the matter.

"Only one thing though," I said, now speaking to Hardwick, "the kid's coloured."

"Well," he replied, without hesitation. "So what has he got against Jews?"

I laughed and relaxed. I should have known better than to mention it, but already something seemed to be rubbing off on me. I was encountering so many fears and prejudices each day that I was now looking for them, peeping under each situation just in case some hidden prejudice was lurking there. I'd have to watch myself. That sort of thing just won't do.

"When do we expect you?" Hannah asked.

"After work this evening," I said. "Seven, seven-thirty, thereabouts. Okay?"

"Fine, see you then. 'Bye."

I had two calls to make in Brixton, so I tidied my desk and went downstairs.

First I went to see a Joshua Roberts, 62 Kingston Park Road, Brixton. There was no answer. I'd written stating the time I'd call. Still no answer. A long journey with a blank at the end of it. Oh well, let's press on.

Second call, Thornton Loomis, 16 Vale Street, Brixton. Let's hope you're home, Mr Loomis. After all, you asked for this visit. His letter had arrived that morning and the Supervisor had passed it on to me. It read:

The Director,
The Welfare Department
Dear Sir,

I am a West Indian from Grenada resident and in employment in London only for the purpose of completing my studies.

I am married with two children under six years, both boys. Recently there have arisen serious domestic differences between my wife and myself, as a result of which it seems more than likely that I will find it necessary to dissolve the home and place the children in an Institution until I am ready to return to Grenada. I would welcome an opportunity for discussing the procedure with a member of your staff.

> I have the honour to be, Sir,
> Yours respectfully,
> THORNTON W. LOOMIS

I must have read the letter several times over, trying to get a mental picture of Mr Loomis. The clear, precise statement of his position and intention seemed to indicate, at least, a good educational background. So I was it, the someone to talk to Mr Thornton W. Loomis.

He answered the door and stood looking at me in open-mouthed surprise.

"Mr Loomis?"

"Yes, I'm Mr Loomis."

"I'm from the Welfare Department."

"But, I thought . . . " he began, not quite knowing what to say. He had not expected someone like me.

"We got your letter and I've come to see if I can help in any way."

"But I didn't know, I mean, I didn't think, I mean . . . "

"I understand, Mr Loomis. Actually I've not been with the Welfare Department very long, you know."

"Anyway, won't you come in?"

He led the way down a short flight of stone stairs into the basement. A largish living-room, nicely furnished and clean. The floor was covered with a gaily patterned carpet in varying shades of red with a leafy motif. On the right of the main entrance double doorways led into what may have been bedrooms. Through the half-open door I caught a glimpse of a small bed. Opposite was another doorway from which came sounds of running water and the rattle of dishes. Two small children were playing at trains on the floor. The train was a straight-backed chair lying on its side; they were having an argument over who should be the driver this time. Ages about three and five.

Mr Loomis led me to an overstuffed settee away from the children.

"Please sit down. I'll tell the wife you're here." He went through the doorway into the room from which came the sounds of water and crockery. After a few minutes he returned. About thirty, five feet eight or thereabouts and thin, with sharp, chiselled features and straight, black hair brushed neatly backward away from his forehead. An intelligent, sensitive face, but slightly womanish, I thought. Indian origin. Neatly dressed in a dark blue suit, white shirt and a University tie.

I took another look at the children. They were lighter skinned than their father, with brownish curling hair, both chubby, well-nourished boys. One of them had a host of freckles on his face. Handsome boys. I wondered what the wife looked like.

"My wife will be with us in a moment," he said. Very formal and distant. Probably disappointed with me. He was all set to receive a white person, and look at what turned up. I'd have to get round that somehow.

"Couple of nice boys," I remarked. "Born here?" I knew they were. Their voices were as English as old Big Ben, but softer. Anyway, it was an opening gambit.

"Oh, yes. Both born here," he replied, giving very little.

"Economics or Law?" I'd try another angle, this time with the tie.

"Economics," he said. "London School of Economics." He said this with pride, placing himself where he belonged. A person of quality.

This was a better start. I asked him about his studies and plans for the future and learned that he intended to return home and go into politics. He asked me about my own work, and for the record I gave him a brief run-down on my life in Britain, watching him—university, the Royal Air Force, schoolmaster, now this. I watched the change happening in his face. He liked the sound of that, the prestige value of famous institutions, the mystique of belonging. Each moment my stock was going up with him. I nearly laughed as I thought that each moment my skin was becoming whiter to him, more acceptable.

"Great," he said, "great. But why are you doing this job?"

"Oh, that's a long story. Maybe one of these days when we have time I'll tell you about it."

He was looking at me now with something near to respect. Then his wife appeared. We both stood up as she came in, drying her hands on her gay, frilly edged apron.

I hope I had enough sense to keep my mouth from gaping. She was a peach, a knockout. Lovely and pink-flushed from the warmth of her efforts in the kitchen. As tall as her husband. Fair and sun-touched, with a mass of tumbling curly brown hair. An oval face out of which her large brown eyes shone darkly, mischievously. No make-up on the full, pouting lips. Beautiful, even teeth, with a glint of gold on one molar. Probably Portuguese, I thought, with other things. A lot of different blood had gone into producing this lovely woman. Her movement towards us was easy and light, flowing from the hips but proud, haughty.

She was dressed in a suit of red linen, short-sleeved, with no ornaments of any kind. Her eyebrows were thick, lustrous and untouched. Some men are born lucky, I thought.

We shook hands. Hers was strong and warmly damp. Her husband may have prepared her for me, because she showed no surprise in her manner. In fact, she seemed pleased.

"Glad to meet you, Mr Braithwaite," she said. I had not yet mentioned my name to either of them.

"I peeked," she continued, laughing. "Recognized you. Saw you on TV last week. Besides, I read your book."

One up to the lady in the red linen suit. Her husband took his cue. "Oh, yes. I heard about you, but I didn't connect the name," he said. "I knew you had joined the Welfare Service," he added. "You mentioned it during the TV programme."

Well, there we were, all nice and cosy and informed. So now we could get on with the business in hand. I noticed that she sat in a chair some distance from her husband, although there was plenty of room beside him where he sat on the settee.

"We received your letter at the office, Mr Loomis," I began, "so I am here to offer any help I can. But first I ought to explain something of my position. Normally we do not interfere in anyone's domestic affairs, but where children are involved we would like to help in any way which would avoid their ever coming into the Council's care. From the tone of your letter it would seem that whatever action you contemplate might possibly affect the children adversely, so I've come along to try to help you sort things out. I'm no specialist in these matters, but I've been in Britain a long time, and my experiences here may be of some use to you."

While I was speaking, his wife was staring at me in wide-eyed surprise. Now she stood up, looking from him to me.

"What letter are you talking about? What's this all about?" And to him: "What on earth have you been up to?"

He became rather flustered and said to her: "Take it easy. I'll explain it to you later." Then to me: "Look, Mr Braithwaite, all I wanted was that the Welfare people would send someone to tell me what would happen to the children in case my wife and I parted, or something like that."

"Thornton!" she exclaimed, the look on her face painful. "You didn't send that letter?"

"I told you I would," he replied.

"But I thought you were joking." Her voice was a sob. The colour had receded from her face, leaving it sickly pale.

I looked at him, sitting there smug and sure of himself, and I had the feeling that this little man was trying to use the Department and me, or whoever had come, in an attempt to frighten his wife, for some reason best known to himself. She turned to me, her lips trembling with anguish and humiliation.

"Mr Braithwaite, will you please tell me what was in the letter my husband wrote to you?"

I looked at him, wondering how I should answer that one. This thing between them was not really my business. Or was it? Play for time, I told myself.

"I would have thought your husband consulted with you before writing it, Mrs Loomis."

"Please, please," she replied. "I don't know anything about it. Last week he made some silly remark about putting the children in a home, but I thought he was teasing."

"You should know me by now," he said. "When I say I'll do a thing, I do it." His remark was both smug and cruel.

"It's not fair," she cried, and covering her face with her apron, she collapsed in her chair.

I began to dislike Mr Loomis. I felt embarrassed and a bit helpless in this situation and I didn't like the feeling one little bit. I didn't like being used this way, by him or anyone. I stood up. If I remained here any longer, chances were I would become angry and maybe take sides. That was not what I was paid to do. "I think I'd better leave you to sort this out between you," I said.

She jumped up, red-eyed but now very angry and determined.

"Oh, no, you don't," she said, her voice quiet but intense. "I don't know what it is my husband has written about me, but whatever it is we're going to have it out here and now. I didn't ask him to send for you, but now that you're here, you're going to stay until I know what's going on." With this, she planted herself firmly between me and the doorway. She looked angry enough to do anything.

"Stop acting the fool and sit down," her husband said, harshly.

She ignored him and remained where she was. This was getting us nowhere. I decided to stay and see it through. I sat down. She walked over and picked up her chair and placed it between me and the door, then sat in it. Evidently she was determined that I should not leave until the matter had been aired.

"Mrs Loomis," I said. "Your husband wrote us stating that there were serious difficulties between you and warned us that he might try to place the children in an Institution."

She was calm now, in complete control of herself. The children went on with their game, happily ignoring us. Her voice was low-pitched but clear and purposeful. "He did, did he? All right. I didn't think he'd ever do something like that to me. It was a mean, dirty trick." She looked directly at him. "And all because of his jealousy. That's all it is, jealousy. He knows it's not true, but he won't let himself believe it's not true."

So she told it, slowly and clearly.

At first, before they were married, she used to think it was nice, his being jealous like that. She was nursing then, at Clapham General Hospital. "I'm from British Guiana. I came over here to study nursing, I met him at a dance during my final year," she explained.

Right from the beginning, he was jealous of everyone she knew, so she had to drop all her friends. According to him, the white men she knew only wanted to use her, and the coloured ones weren't good enough. Only him. She supposed it felt good having someone feel that way about her.

After she finished her finals they were married. They had a little money and bought this house, on a mortgage. He was studying at the Polytechnic then, in the evenings, and working on the Underground during the day. They rented the rooms and flats upstairs and he stopped working to give more time to his studies.

"From the time we were married he wouldn't let me talk to anyone as long as it was a man; not even the friends I knew before I met him. Especially Negroes. He dislikes them, thinks he's above them. He won't rent a room to a Negro, only Indians like himself or white people.

"Even the people who live in this house I mustn't talk to, and all day long he's with his books, so I mustn't disturb him. Sometimes in the afternoon I'd take the boys into the park to play. The other day a young man passed by and admired the boys, then spoke to me for a few minutes, you know, telling me about his own children or something like that. Thornton was coming out to meet me and must have seen me talking to the young man who went off before he arrived. He began asking me all kinds of questions about him, and wouldn't believe that I'd never seen the young man before, or even knew his name."

It had been like that ever since. They never went anywhere because he claimed he was too busy studying, and he wouldn't let her go anywhere by herself. Not even to the cinema. When she went shopping he watched the time, and if she was a little late he hinted that perhaps she had met somebody, some man or other.

"Do you know what it's been like for me these past four years? Cooped up in these two rooms day and night? Well, I got fed up with it and recently I've been going off to the cinema in the afternoons with the children. So naturally he says I've been meeting a man. He's even been questioning the children about me, trying to get them to say something. Then he began threatening to take them away. I just don't know what's the matter with him. I think he ought to see a doctor or something." She paused, breathing deeply.

"Two weeks ago he began sleeping out here, on the settee. So I thought if that's the way he wants it, that's fine with me. And when I didn't go to him, he said it was because there was some other man, so I didn't need him any more. That's all he does, day and night, hints and accusations, until I'm fed up to here." She put her right hand to her throat.

"He said he'd tell the Welfare people to come and take the children because I was not fit to care for them, but I thought he was joking. I didn't think he'd really do it, not really." Her face crumpled, and she covered it with her hands, sobbing pitifully.

I was enraged. I would have liked to take Mr Bigshot Loomis by the throat and shake the life out of him. But all I did was sit there while she sobbed and he watched her, his face cold and expressionless. The boys had stopped their game and now ran to their mother, their faces frightened, and hung on to her, hiding their curly heads in her lap. They, too, were crying, not understanding, but in sympathy with her, and responding to the fear of something beyond their grasp.

"My wife doesn't understand," Mr Loomis said. "I'm merely trying to keep her out of trouble. I know what men are and I don't want her to get mixed up in anything. I came to Britain to study and qualify, and I intend to do just that and keep myself to myself. I know what West Indians are like and I don't want her mixing with any of them. As soon as I take my finals, we're leaving for home."

He had it worked out very neatly.

"And meanwhile, what about your wife and children?" I asked.

"What do you mean?" he asked. "I'm taking care of them, aren't I? They're comfortable here, and she gets enough each month to run the house and pay for everything. All the rent that comes in from upstairs I turn over to her, because I've got enough to do with my studies. What more does she want?

"I've told her I don't want any men hanging around her. She's married and that should be enough for her. I don't want her mixing with all kinds of people. This is not our country, and we've got to keep to ourselves. She's got enough to do taking care of the children."

She straightened up, rubbing her eyes. "Mr Braithwaite, do you know he won't even let the boys play with the neighbour's children? The only time they get out of here is when I take them out. I tell him they need to play with children their own age, but he won't listen.

"He's full of jealousy and prejudice, that's his trouble. We have an empty room upstairs and last Friday a young African came to inquire about it. Thornton had gone to the tobacconist for cigarettes so I asked the young man to come in and wait. Do you know, he won't rent the room to him. Just because he's a Negro. He doesn't like Negroes. Anyone would think he was white, the way he carries on. Do you know what he said to me when he came to the kitchen just now? He said, 'there's a black fellow outside from the Welfare Office'. That's what he said. Although he's dark himself he seems to hate dark people. Maybe he only married me because I'm fair."

She laid it all right on the line. He'd asked for it and now he'd got it.

"Maybe," she continued, "the best thing for me is to take the children home with me to British Guiana, don't you think? I can stay with my parents until he qualifies and is ready to return. But I don't want to remain here like this any more."

He said nothing. I wondered what he was thinking in that handsome well-shaped head of his. Poor bastard, I thought. You're not big enough inside of you to cope with this beautiful woman. Not nearly big enough to appreciate your good fortune. What she said about him not liking Negroes was his affair. Maybe he didn't even like himself very much. And he had hopes of going into politics? Some hope. But then again, maybe he'd make it. Maybe there was a set-up in Grenada which would suit him, or else he'd go somewhere where the political climate favoured his type of thinking. Probably somewhere like British Guiana where he could join in the Negro versus Indian tug-of-war. To hell with him, I thought. She'd fight him. He'd never break her spirit. I'd just let him know how the land lay as far as I, as a Welfare Officer, was concerned. The black fellow from the Welfare Office.

"Mrs Loomis, I cannot advise you in the matter of your relationship with your husband. But I must make one thing clear. The Department will not consider taking over the care of children in circumstances such as these. If you find difficulty in straightening out your marital difficulties, there are agencies and people well qualified to help and advise you, much more than I could."

Suddenly it occurred to me that I was slipping up on this job. I was here to help, and the nature of that help should be in terms of the existing difficulties. At least I should try, not back away mouthing a lot of evasive claptrap. Sure, the situation was a bit outside my experience, but if I wanted to learn how to serve, how to be helpful, then I had to learn in the best of possible ways, by doing.

"Look, Mr Braithwaite," Loomis said. "Selma doesn't understand, but I do. In this country it's unwise for dark-skinned people to make themselves too conspicuous, you know. No one would know that Selma isn't white, but the children and myself, that's different. I try to explain this to her. When we get back home we can go out and entertain, and do all sorts of things, because we'll be among our own people. But, over here, the best thing for us to do is keep ourselves to ourselves."

I was beginning to get the picture now. Something, some time, had either hurt or badly frightened this little man, and he was on the retreat.

"So meanwhile you intend to hide yourself away, you and your family, like invisible people," I asked.

"All I intend to do is mind my own business," he said firmly.

"You are an intelligent man, Mr Loomis," I said, "and I feel sure that you may have very good reasons for wanting to hide yourself away, to mind your own business, as you say. But I'd like to suggest one thing to you. Your usefulness when you return to Grenada would be very much greater if your experience of life in Britain was as wide as you could make it. After all, Grenada is a very mixed society. As a leader, you will be expected to deal with all kinds of persons. Then, purely for political reasons, it might be a good thing to understand as much as you can about many kinds of people before returning to Grenada."

It occurred to me that this might be a good line to take with this ambitious little man.

"Here in England you have a wonderful opportunity at close hand for learning about people. Many of the problems you will find in Grenada have their counterpart here, and more than that, you will be able here to learn about new pressures and tensions long before they do appear on the scene in Grenada. But you cannot learn these things if you shut yourself away from contact with others.

"With your intelligence and ambition, it would be silly to be afraid of people. If you spend from three to five years here being afraid, you might find it difficult to lose the habit when you return home. You cannot live in a state of suspension here and then expect to behave like a responsible person later. You've got to stop being afraid and begin being responsible."

"Oh, I'm not afraid of anyone," he boasted.

"I'm not the one you need to convince of that, Mr Loomis," I replied. "You'll have to prove that to your wife, and even more to yourself. Later on you might find it necessary to prove it to those two sons of yours."

He licked his lip, the first sign of nervousness he had shown. Maybe I was getting to him, touching on his vanity. Now that Mrs Loomis was again composed, the boys returned to their game, quickly forgetful in the more serious business of deciding whose turn it now was to be driver.

"But I don't know many people," he said. "I sometimes meet some fellows, you know, West Indians, at L.S.E. and we talk over coffee, but that's about all."

"Well," I added, "why not begin with them? Invite a few here for a chat, and get to know them. You've a nice place here, and it might give your wife something to do, entertaining your friends, sort of in preparation for her future role as Governor's wife in Grenada."

We both laughed at this.

"Well, it could happen, you know," he said. A real go-getter, this boy.

"Sure it could happen," I agreed, "but you'd have to begin now to make it happen by preparing for it. Already you have most of the ingredients, a lovely wife, a nice house, your studies, your ambitions. Sure it could happen. All you need now is to stop being afraid. Of other men." I added the last bit harshly, to shake him up. He took it with a smile. I looked at his wife. She was watching him, too, her face relaxed but ready to take a cue from his attitude.

"I suppose you're right," he said. "All this may have seemed silly to you, but . . . "

"Not silly, Mr Loomis," I interrupted. "If I had been married to such a lovely woman I might have behaved a lot worse, a whole lot worse." I sneaked a quick look at her; she was smiling shyly. "However, you're the one who's going to be the politician, not me. So you'll have to learn to handle all kinds of opposition."

"You make it sound so damned easy," he replied, then, "Sorry, Selma." 'Good grief,' I thought, 'he'd write a letter like that about her, but he apologizes to her for saying "damn". Wonders never cease. Or maybe he was saying "sorry" for something else.'

"Could you stay for a cup of tea?" she asked, rising.

"Of course," I replied. "Me, I'm dry. It's people like your husband here who have to learn to talk for hours without lubrication."

He laughed. We all laughed. Nice and friendly. They'd work it out together, I felt sure. I'd put a little idea in his head and he'd use it. Ambitious types like him would use anything to achieve their ends. Inwardly I wished them luck, especially him. In one way he'd need it, lots of it.

Over tea, the three of us chatted, chiefly about Mr Loomis and his political ambitions, and then, with a promise to drop in any time I was in the vicinity, I left them.

The Rosenbergs lived in a large apartment house overlooking Clapham Common, close to the building where Wilberforce and his friends often met to discuss their schemes for bringing about the emancipation of the slaves in British territories. They were both restless, energetic, brilliant people, pursuing their separate careers, together with their joint career of involvement in a host of projects and schemes for helping a wide assortment of social misfits to help themselves. Their apartment was a kind of crossroads, where all kinds of personalities and intelligences met, talked, ate, argued, agreed or disagreed, but rarely rested. The need to understand and cope with urgent human problems seemed to outweigh the need for rest. Sometimes one slept if one had to, and then this was respected and the wakeful, restless ones moved themselves off to the kitchen, bathroom, bedroom or distant corner, and carried on in what they thought were whispers. Their little Clarita, their daughter of three, bobbed about like a small cork on the turbulences of the grown-up world in which she lived; her large, steady grey eyes and serious mien would soon discourage the uninitiated who tried to woo her with baby talk, but would just as readily crinkle up in the most captivating way when she was amused.

Hardwick answered the door. When indoors he always dressed his tall, gangling frame in thick, chunky sweaters and shapeless corduroy slacks. His greying hair pointed in every direction under the persistent teasing of his restless fingers, as he read, argued or concentrated on problems new or past. Under a large, craggy forehead, his aquiline nose, brown, slightly bulging eyes and wide full-lipped mouth usually gave the impression of professorial ponderousness until he smiled, releasing an irrepressible boyishness. He loved to joke, but invariably in the most unbelievably corny way, so that one was tickled into laughter, not at the content of the joke, but at his crass temerity in hoping for what he invariably got—laughter.

"Hey, Hannah," he called. "Rick's here." He and I went into the sitting-room and made ourselves comfortable, and were soon joined by Hannah, his wife. Theirs may have been the attraction of opposites, for she was small, blonde and well-formed. Her most outstanding characteristic was not in any physical feature, but in the aura of dynamic energy which surrounded her, whether at home, at a tame social gathering, or on the concert platform where she repeatedly astounded her audience by the amazing dexterity of those small, flexible hands.

"Come on, tell us about him," she said, without preamble.

I told them about little Roddy; all his history as was known or surmised. Then I described the boy, and it may well be that my description reflected my own enthusiasm. At the end of my recital, Hardwick said: "What about the wings?"

"What wings?" I asked, not getting it.

"An angel he describes, and wings he forgets!" At his corniest Hardwick was prone to imitate the Jewish stereotype.

"Give him time," I said, "they'll grow."

"What do you think?" he asked his wife.

"Okay with me," she replied. "The only problem here is how the most important person will react to the idea."

"My guess is that he'll like you both very much." I said.

"Sorry," she answered. "I meant the other important person. Clarita. Everything will depend on how well they get on."

"Of course," I agreed, and went on to explain the carefully planned sequence in all arrangements for fostering or adoption.

First: To find prospective parents and discuss the case with them, giving them as much as was known of the child, his parents, if any, and background.

Second: The parents make formal application, for fostering or adoption, on prepared forms, giving details of themselves, their occupations, domestic arrange ments, financial circumstances, references, *et al.*

Third: The parents were taken to the Home and intro
    duced to the new child. In each case the parents saw
    only the child concerned, as it was very necessary
    to avoid the temptation to choose one from several
    likely candidates.
Fourth: If this introduction went well, the parents visited
    again, this time together with any child or children of
    their own. The youngsters were given the opportunity
    to meet, play together for a while, and size each other
    up.
Fifth: Providing all went well so far, the fosteree or adoptee
    was taken for visits to his new home. These were
    progressive, beginning with a visit of a few hours
    one afternoon and gradually extending to a weekend,
    then perhaps a week. Then, if all parties were satisfied,
    on a subsequent visit the child would merely stay with
    the family, with no fuss or bother.

We discussed the matter fully, and when I was sure that they were really enthusiastic about the idea, I brought up the fact of Roddy's colour, and, in the event of his becoming a part of their family, the difficulties which might later have to be faced.

"You've forgotten one thing, Rick," Hardwick said, when I had finished. "If the boy becomes a member of this family, that's just what he will be. Whatever difficulties, as you call them, are to be faced, will be faced by us as a family. Enough said?"

"Enough said," I replied.

This was the sort of remark and these the sort of people who helped to sustain my faith in mankind; a faith which, during my life in Britain, had often deserted me. This was a Jewish couple, but so complete was their involvement with all humanity that neither of them had asked any question about the child's religion or that of his parents, if it was known. The fact that they were Jews was very much secondary to the fact that they were human beings.

I always carried some of the application forms in my brief case, and now they completed one of these, with a certain amount of ribaldry over some of the details.

The train ride home to Ilford was long, with several changes, and it was with a grateful feeling of something accomplished that I finally crawled into bed.

Chapter
Four

MERELY FOR A CHANGE in the dull, daily routine of riding the Underground to work all the way, I came out at Mile End Station, caught a bus for the rest of the journey, and climbed to the upper deck. It was crowded, but I saw an empty place on one of the two front seats and squeezed my way there. When I had settled myself I noticed that the person sitting beside me was a Negro. His face was turned towards the windows on his side, as if he were deeply interested in the drab sameness of the scene which flitted by. Anyway, I said "Hello, there," and he quickly turned and smiled, as if he had been waiting for a signal from me before even acknowledging my presence. This did not surprise me, because it was one of the things I had been learning about Negroes in Britain, especially Negroes from the West Indies.

In their sunsplashed islands, West Indian Negroes are generally gay, friendly, talkative people, accustomed to greeting each other, whether stranger or friend, with a wave, a nod, a wink, or

"Hi, man". They see each other, look each other in the face in hope of recognizing someone from the same town, village, street, school, or place of employment, and if on another island, they look into each other's faces in the hope of recognizing someone from home.

In Britain, they behave quite differently. They very rarely look another strange Negro in the face, and yet, should one be bold enough to offer the old familiar "Hi there" or "Hi, man," the reaction is immediately friendly, as if there is always the hope of being addressed, though veiled by the seeming preoccupation with something else. I have seen this phenomenon very often, and conclude that it is part of the plurality of artifices behind which Negroes in Britain are prone to hide in attempting to evade the manifold face of prejudice. For they frequently find prejudice within their own ranks, brought along with them to Britain to add to the difficulties against which they constantly declaim.

Although circumscribed, as a group, by the anti-Negro prejudice which shows itself in a variety of ways, they still find time and energy to maintain among themselves the invidious demarcations between manual worker, office worker and student groups; between dark-skinned and light-skinned; between the educated and the unlettered. As a result, they remain dislocated, scattered, leaderless and voiceless, without any positive organization or representation, in spite of the many able and talented ones to be found, at all levels, among them.

In times of crisis, they mill madly around, striking out blindly against the common enemy, but at the same time fighting among themselves for the elusive laurels of leadership. But as soon as the high point of the crisis is past they quickly revert to self-interest, loquaciously against any suggestion of unified, positive action to establish that group dignity without which all their efforts are largely in vain. At the drop of a hat, or even before, they would engage each other on their favourite topic, racial prejudice in Britain; yet any suggestion that they shoulder some of the responsibility for improvement in inter-racial relationship receives the stock answer, "What can we do in this white man's country?"

The manual workers give their attention and time to earning enough to provide food, clothing, shelter and 'something to put by' against that glorious day when they can shake the dust of Britain forever from their feet. They live with high hopes that that day would easily be realized in five, seven or ten years of careful living and saving, but often discover to their cost that they had not taken into account one factor which very often wrecks their most careful plans; the rapacity of landlords, *many of them Negroes,* who take full advantage of the prevailing anti-Negro prejudice in housing accommodation, and mercilessly bleed the unfortunate immigrant in the filthy, overcrowded slum ghettos which are generally the only places open to them.

The office worker very often has deliberately cast himself adrift from the West Indies and has no intention of returning there. Usually of middle-class West Indian stock, he retains his many middle-class West Indian prejudices, and wants little else than to settle down eventually in middle-class British surroundings, and increase the areas of difference between him and the manual workers with whom he claims to have very little in common.

The student groups are separate from both of these, but among them are two main striations of studentship; bona-fide full-time students who may be supported by wealthy parents or grant-aided by Government scholarships; and the part-time worker-students at various stages of study and at any age from twenty to fifty or over. They spend periods of from one to five years or longer in Britain, preparing for the day of triumphant return home with the 'open sesame'. They are readily articulate about prejudice in Britain, and claim to know exactly what should be done to bring about a change in the inter-racial status quo. But they themselves do nothing and excuse themselves either with the ready-made device of claiming pressure of academic work (an excuse which seems strangely inadequate when it is noticed how much time they can spare to meet and discuss what ought to be done, by someone else) or by insisting that they are transients and therefore free of any responsibility for action, either on their own account, or on behalf of others.

This is especially true of the law students, and other embryonic political leaders. They dilate at length on the million and one injustices perpetrated by colonialists, and quote chapter and verse of historical data to back up their statements. They claim to know exactly what must be done to improve conditions in the separate West Indian islands, and to make the idea of a Federal entity become an effective reality. They talk glibly about leadership, but studiously avoid any contact with the open opportunities available at close hand for practical exercise in the things they talk about.

They avoid the workers, and the workers, in turn, despise them and consider them little better than erudite windbags. Having at close hand observed the snooty, supercilious attitude of many of these people, I once suggested that because many of them have their scholarship grants paid out of taxes collected from these sweat-grimed workers, they should be required to give a little of their time, a few days each year, in social work, as a small token return. It might help them to appreciate the relationship between them and those less fortunate than themselves. Each year, West

Indian immigrants in Britain send more than a million pounds sterling back to the West Indies as savings or aid to relatives they left behind; if it were possible to keep close track of this money, I am sure it would be discovered that some of it found its way eventually into the pockets of these grant-aided students who so readily dismiss their unlettered brethren as being several miles beneath their contempt.

But for worker and student the main preoccupation is invisibility. They go to and from college or place of employment fully retracted within themselves, their eyes seeing but not seeing, their ears deaf to everything which is not intimately related to work and home. Their chief concern is to be unobserved, like blank spaces in the ranks of white men. Yet in the very act of hiding, they are acutely conscious of the presence of discrimination and prejudice and embittered by the deep assaults made on their dignity. This is further complicated by the knowledge of conditions 'back home', and the unhappy comparisons which this produces.

Perhaps, for the first time in his life the new citizen is in regular employment, receiving a wage which allows him to pay for his everyday needs, enjoy some of the things which had hitherto seemed beyond his reach, make a small regular saving, and send something back home to help a needy relative or pay off the instalments of money borrowed to make the trip. Perhaps, for the first time in his life he is free of the fear of illness and unemployment and the threat of debt or death with which these were previously associated. And perhaps, for the first time in his life, he owns something, a house, a car, a radio or TV set, or maybe a bed, but something, and this is important. Therefore he is preoccupied with keeping himself to himself, to have and to hold what he has, and to expose himself as little as possible to anything which might take it away from him. Social benefits, whether in the form of Old Age pensions, unemployment or maternity payments, or educational facilities for his children are accepted and exploited as fully as possible, but generally from the position of outsiders benefiting by accident, rather than as citizens participating in a progressive social evolution; and, as outsiders, when hurt by indignity or malpractice, they make no positive, collective protest, but withdraw farther and farther within their unhappy caves of bitterness and despair.

The young man beside me was talking.

"Working around here?"

"Yes," I replied, "on the other side of the river, Brixton way."

"You're lucky," he said. "I'm going to the Labour Exchange, but I know it's a waste of time; yet if I don't go, that's always the time somebody says they were taking on men."

"How long have you been out of work?"

"Nearly ten weeks. Every day it's the same. Nothing today. Nothing today. All the time you see the notices up with jobs. Jobs, jobs, jobs and every one of them with the f—ing N.C. on it. The white men don't want the jobs, but still they write the f—ing N.C. on them." His voice became flat with hate. "You know what I think, pal? I think they don't really have any jobs. I think they just make up those cards and put the N.C. on them just to show us that they think we're shit. That's what it is. Just to let us read it and know they don't want us. Christ! I'd like to take all those cards and stuff them up their ass."

As he spoke I was watching his face, the stark, bitter hatred I saw there. At first sight he had seemed nondescript in a black-dyed ex-Army greatcoat and a soft cloth cap pulled low over his eyes, hiding most of his face. But now, his eyes were narrowed and glinting, and his features pressed into a sharp vindictive mask. I could find no words to say to him, nothing strong enough, honest enough, or meaningful enough to offer against the simple rightness of his hatred.

He wanted so desperately to preserve his dignity and manhood, and at every step he was being thwarted until all he had left was his hate. I knew what the N.C. meant. NO COLOURED. And whether they realized it or not, it also meant NO CHRISTIAN, because most West Indians are very religious people. Two little letters at the end of an advertisement, and yet they could produce such cumulative bitterness. But the greatest irony lay in the fact that the Labour Exchanges are Government Offices of the Ministry of Labour, and it is inescapable that Her Majesty's Government is either being crudely exploited to put a respectable face on these unliberal practices, or is deliberately participating in such a foul act of blatant discrimination to serve its own ends.

As if to add insult to injury, unemployment benefits are often paid in the same Labour Exchanges, which accept the fact that there is employment, and equally accept the prohibitions against the coloured person seeking employment; then pay him maintenance because he is unemployed. It seems to me that any employer who has the gall to submit such a flagrant prohibition should be made to pay maintenance to every applicant turned down because of it.

This young Negro felt that he had every reason to be bitter. What could I say to him? Could I pontificate about hate being useless and wasteful of energy? Could I say anything to him about personal responsibility which would not, in the circumstances, sound banal and false? I was on my way to a warm office, with desk and telephone and the morning cup of coffee, and respectful colleagues, and a sure salary cheque each month, and, and . . . What could I say to him which would give him the feeling that I really cared, and understood, and sympathized? The bus arrived at my destination and I bade him goodbye, leaving him wrapped up in his oversize coat, his pulled down cap and his misery. But I took with me a recurrent echo of his voice.

In writing it down now, I am putting it as I remember it, as I understood it. His speech was not polished or grammatical, and he used many words which, by themselves, were unfamiliar to me. But there was no mistaking the power and clarity of his meaning, the vehemence and incisiveness of his hatred. As they came out of him, forceful and elementally crude, they seemed right for the thing he felt, the only honest vehicle for the fearsome blackness growing within him. They did not defile him. I wondered if any of the many passengers on the bus would see the slim figure, or the half-veiled face, and have any suspicion of the truly frightening thing within him, for the presence of which they were all equally culpable. No, that was not quite right, *we* were all equally culpable, because there was no easing off my part of the blame. I, too, had a responsibility for the loathsome indignity under which this young man and others like him were being casually crushed each day, and my responsibility was the greater because I knew, at first-hand experience, what it was like.

I had reached the point, so far, of convincing myself that I had put every vestige of bitterness and racial hatred behind me, yet now, after little more than two minutes with a complete stranger, I felt it again inside me, clamouring for attention. He was black and so was I, and I experienced an immediate identity with him and his hurts, because I knew that to most of the other passengers, and equally, to most other Britons, he and I were equally two black faces, indistinguishable, despised, rejected and ignored. And if I went along to the Labour Exchange, I would be treated to the same exposure. N.C.

Holy Christ! And people talk of peace. And they talk of freedom. Freedom from what? and for what? In my heart I wanted to be free of bitterness and hatred and spite towards anyone, irrespective of his ethnic markings. But how could I ever be free when all around me was evidence of the enchainment of myself? If he suffers, then I also suffer; if he is spat on, then I am also spat on, and my fancy suit, and shiny shoes, and comfortable home will not make any of it easier to bear. And if he could hate so deeply and completely, then God help me, I had better watch myself day and night, hour by hour, lest I give way to what must be just as surely fermenting in me. Was this what the colleagues meant whenever they said, "your people . . . "? Could they see, beyond the dark skins, the other identities?

At the office I prepared my report on Roddy Williams, detailing my visits to all the people concerned in the case, and adding my own recommendations. I stressed the facts that the boy was born in Britain, knew no other language or associations, and had spent all his life with white persons. It therefore seemed most natural to me that I should try to place him with a white family, as there were so very many common factors already established. To this report I added the completed application form from the Rosenbergs, commenting on my own knowledge of them and my opinion as to their suitability as foster-parents. I placed all this in the case folder and sent it to the Supervisor.

Most of the morning was spent on preparing reports on visits; in the afternoon I would be beginning on another of my tough cases.

When I returned from lunch there was a note on my desk asking me to see the Supervisor at 2 p.m. that afternoon. She greeted me with a charming smile and, sitting down, I noticed that she had been reading the Williams case.

"I see you've been getting on with the Williams file," she remarked. Although I had put it all down in the file, I nevertheless gave her a quick résumé of my activities.

"Do you know the Rosenbergs very well?"

"Yes," I replied, "they are friends of mine."

"I should think they are quite well off and very intelligent," she observed. I waited to see where it would lead. "I'm sure you have studied the boy's background very carefully."

"Oh, yes," I replied. "I've also checked in every way I could."

"Mr Braithwaite, in view of this child's background, I do not think that sort of home would be quite suitable for him. It seems to me that we should try to find him a home where the intellectual atmosphere would be, shall we say, less demanding."

When I finally found my voice, I said: "I'm afraid I don't quite understand you, Miss Wren."

"I'm thinking about the boy's mother and father," she continued, with cool imperturbability. "It would be unwise of us to ignore the important effects of heredity in these matters."

She was talking about a boy not yet five years old, whom all who knew him described as intelligent. He had never lived with his parents, and knew neither of them. But the whore-Mexican tag seemed to have dug really deep. I, too, remembered it, but I wanted to fight against it.

"I don't believe any of that as applied to this boy," I said, somewhat heatedly. "I've seen him. And I know the Rosenbergs. The atmosphere does not disturb their child and it won't disturb Roddy.

They are intelligent people and kind with it. In that sort of atmosphere the boy would have a real chance to develop, and they'd encourage him. I can't see why his unfortunate first choice of parents should be held against him."

"I'm not holding anything against him, I'm merely facing the facts. In this work we cannot afford mistakes which will have disastrous effects on the lives of the children whom it is our business to help and protect."

"But would it have mattered if his mother had been a princess and his father a bank president?" I asked angrily.

"It might," she replied. "Your tendency to ignore these important things and your inclination to dismiss them as trivial may be due to your lack of formal training in this field. Frankly speaking, your concern for these children is no greater than mine, than ours."

"And frankly speaking," I replied, seizing on this opening, "I think that it is. The idea that the princeling brought up in the gamekeeper's hut nevertheless behaves in a princely way belongs to the realm of fairy tales; similarly, the veiled suggestions and hints that this child has bad blood which must necessarily out. Maybe my lack, as you call it, of formal training helps me to concern myself more with doing than with finding reasons why things should not or could not be done. I have seen this child, and I think he is right for this family."

I must hand it to her. Not by a flicker of an eyelash did she indicate impatience, or anger, or anything. I'm sure she didn't learn that at the place where she received the oft-praised formal training. This came from a long history of being superior and refusing to be controlled by a situation.

"About these friends of yours," she gave the 'friends' heavy inflexion. "I see they are Jewish."

"Yes," I replied.

"That's unfortunate," she said. "We would be sure to run into a lot of difficulty from Jewish adoption organizations on that score. Apart from that, it might be very unwise to put the boy in a Jewish home and the different religious circumstances which go with it."

I could only look at her in wonderment. Wasn't the fact of their willingness to give the child a home sufficiently important to stimulate any enthusiasm in her? They had not let their Jewishness or his Gentileness enter into their thinking, so why should we?

"Miss Wren, little Roddy hasn't any religion, or if he has nobody has yet mentioned it, besides nobody has mentioned whether or not his mother is Jewish or Gentile, probably because her being a prostitute was sufficiently damning. Even his father might be Jewish; there are Jews in Mexico too, I suppose. But all this is, to me, very much like red herrings—rotten red herrings which will not help this child one tiny bit. This case was turned over to me because nobody was making progress with it. Luckily I've found somewhere for him, or I think I have. Don't you want the boy to get out of that Institution? Or do you think that a white home is too good for him?" I had forgotten to be careful and polite.

"It's not just this child, Mr Braithwaite. It's all of them. In this work we must be careful to avoid any criticism which would hurt not just one case, but the whole department." She pressed a little white button on her desk, then continued: "We cannot rush headlong into these matters, and after you have been with the Department a while longer you will understand the justice of our system."

There was a discreet knock on the door and it opened. She came into the room, a large, greying, comfortable person. That was the word which always came into my mind whenever I saw the Deputy Chief. Comfortable. It would not be difficult to imagine her seated in a large armchair by a roaring fire, surrounded by a whole regiment of sons and daughters and grandchildren. She always moved gracefully, as if accustomed to doing the right thing in the right way. Her face was round and pleasant, but the pale blue eyes were steady and suggested prudent strength.

"Oh, do come in, Miss Whitney," the Chief said. "Mr Braithwaite and I have been discussing the case of the little Williams boy."

Miss Whitney smiled and nodded, but said nothing. Evidently she knew all about it and had come in to reinforce the Chief's position. Well, she didn't need to. If they wanted the kid to stay in the Home, that was up to them.

"I've been explaining to him the difficulties which we can expect to crop up from the fact that the persons he has recommended as foster-parents are Jewish, but I think he is inclined to be somewhat impatient with me."

"True," Miss Whitney agreed, "we'll have to be ready to meet quite a few objections from various quarters, but I think you can say it won't be the first time." She smiled.

I started. It sounded as if they were for the idea, not against it. I stared at them, and said to Miss Wren: "But I thought you were against this whole thing?"

"Not against it; oh, no. I'm very pleased that you have been able to find a possible family so quickly. But I must make sure that you understand what you're doing and why you're doing it. I wanted to find out whether your interest in the case was merely sentimental because the child is coloured."

"For these children who have spent all their lives in a public institution," Miss Whitney intervened, "we try to ensure that every possible eventuality is covered before the move instead of risking a breakdown and the resultant unhappiness to the child."

I nodded in agreement.

"One thing I must tell you," Miss Wren said. "Because the Rosenbergs are personal friends of yours, some other Welfare Officer will have to take over the case from this point. That's to make sure that the relationship between the Welfare Officer and the prospective family is not so intimate as to destroy his objectivity. This in no way reflects adversely on you, it is merely a matter of policy, and I'm sure you will accept it in that light. I think the best thing for me to do is get in touch with the Area Office nearest to where the Rosenbergs live and have someone from there get in touch with the Rosenbergs. You will, however, be kept informed on developments."

I left her office feeling rather relieved, but still a little bothered by an indefinable something in our relationship which seemed to set us so easily in opposition to each other. Maybe it was me, impatient in my enthusiasm to get on with the job, and irritated by her casual aloofness, especially when I thought I was breaking all kinds of new ground. Back at my desk I sat for a while trying to let the residual irritations pass from me. The office was very quiet.

I settled down to read through the pile of case folders on my desk; a selection of tough cases. They all involved coloured children and their parents, (if any) and had come in from several districts. Part of my job was to break these hard cases wherever possible. It was supposed, (and at first I shared this view) that, being a Negro, I would be able to take a fresh view of each case and from the many points of identity between myself and other coloured persons discover some factor which would prove to be the necessary 'open sesame'. After some months on the job I had learnt that whenever I was successful in helping to resolve a certain situation, it was not because of the colour of my skin, because

I was quickly learning that persons in trouble, no matter what their race or religion, react favourably to a courteous, helpful and really sympathetic approach which respects their dignity while seeking to serve them. I had, in fact, to learn to be colour blind while learning how to serve.

These case sheets made interesting reading; they related to boys and girls all living in Children's Homes and cared for by the Council, their ages ranging from about two to thirteen years. Most of them had been completely abandoned, the others had one or more parents who showed occasional interest in them, but for some reason did not, or could not, remove them from the Home. I chuckled rather audibly as I noticed the way in which reference to the children's origin varied as each Welfare Officer tied her own label to her own case.

Coloured
Black
Negroid
Half-African
Half-Indian
Anglo-Indian
Half-West Indian
Half-Negro
Half-Asian

Odd how the emphasis was always on the child's blackness. Maybe one of these days I will see the term Half-White. Could be that will mean something.

"What's amusing you, Braithwaite?"

E. R. BRAITHWAITE

Jim Baxter must have noticed me grinning to myself. He was one of the five male Welfare Officers in a staff of sixteen. He and I shared the same office with seven female officers, and, not accidentally, our desks were next to each other. Jim had been a Welfare Officer for about six years. Short and slim, with a round boyish face, he knew the book of rules backwards and never took a single step unless he was quite sure of all the precedents. He could quote chapter and verse of Council regulations at the drop of a hat and was fond of using all kinds of bits of technical terms. He knew all the different types of neuroses by name, and after he had interviewed an applicant, would neatly fit him or her into the appropriate neurotic pigeonhole. He never said 'child' if he could say 'sibling'. Jim said he understood the common man because he got his Diploma in Sociology the hard way, night school after a long day's work. Jim said he entertained no colour prejudice because one of his best friends was a Negro. Not me, some other fortunate fellow. Jim said that the British Government should undertake a lot of major work projects in the West Indies, and other overseas territories; then the immigrants would all return home and there would be no colour problem in Britain. Jim was very knowledgeable.

"Something in these files amuses me," I replied, "the way a child is a child, except when he is not a white child."

"Come again." He twisted his face into an expression of mock alarm. "Say that piece of double-Dutch again."

"I'm reading these files, and the children are all half something or other; the white children I deal with are only Tom Brown or Judy White. But these others are all labelled 'Paul Green, half-African' or 'Mary Blue, half-West Indian'. Do you know, this tells me as much about the Welfare Officers as it does about the children."

"How's that?"

"I think these terms indicate that we ourselves are too obsessed with the colour of these children and that may be part of the reason why these cases are still hanging fire. All these children need foster-parents or adoptive parents, but I have the idea that this labelling of them sets up a kind of blockage in the minds of the Welfare Officers which subconsciously inhibits our efforts on the child's behalf."

"That's a lot of nonsense," Jim said. "It's merely a means of letting us know who's who. No sense in trying to have a child fostered or adopted unless you know everything about him."

"In that case we need to be consistent," I replied, thumbing through some papers on my desk. "Here's a case I dealt with last week. Mother—German, father—Irish, Name: Helmut O'Shea, but nothing about his being half-German or half-Irish. So the Welfare Officers can go right ahead and work towards finding him a place in a family. But the half-Negro child is seen as a problem even before the officer begins to operate."

"Come off it, Braithwaite," he said, with an expansive gesture. "You're making something out of nothing. These descriptions are merely for our information, so we know who and what the child is, and the right sort of foster-parent to find for it. We've got to match the child with the parent, you now."

"That does not explain anything," I retorted, "because in each case the Welfare Officer sees the child concerned. We're not working in the dark. If you know the child is dark-skinned does it matter where his parents came from? And if somebody wants either to adopt or foster a child, that person may be willing to take any child, providing it is sound in mind and body."

"Boy, oh boy!" he exclaimed. "How green you are. It's not as easy as all that. The reason why so many coloured children remain year after year in the Council's care is because not many white people will come forward to foster them. Sometimes, you get the odd type who thinks it might be fun to be foster-parent to a black baby, you know, like having a black doll to cuddle and dress up, but they forget that the baby will one day grow up to adolescence, and that's when the problems really begin. We've got to explain this to them and you'd be amazed at how soon many of them change their minds. That's why we're hoping that you will be able to find some foster-parents among the coloured people."

"Seems to me that if any white person showed a wish to foster or adopt a coloured child, our first step should be to encourage instead of frightening them off with talk of problems and adolescence. These things can be handled in either a positive or negative way. You have just described the negative way. I think I would be inclined to encourage the prospective foster-parent to see the child's need for what all children need, love, security, help and encouragement, emphasizing the similarities between the coloured child and his white counterpart. I would help them to understand that all children pass through difficult periods during growth and development, and that a coloured child's problems need be no greater."

"And suppose something happened later on in that child's life? Suppose it didn't work out the way you hoped. What then?" he asked.

"We are not expected to anticipate the future. Our business is to help, to help in every way to make these relationships work. But we must first ourselves believe that there is nothing essentially different between people; I think these labels are here in these files because we are too concerned with differences. I'd like to see them dropped."

"You know something, chum?" he remarked. "You're new to this job. The system was devised by people who know their stuff.

My advice to you is that you wait until you've been here as long as some of us before you begin criticizing things," and with that he turned his attention to his own files.

My first step was always to discuss each case with the Welfare Officer who had previously dealt with it and then, wherever possible, start again from the beginning. Experiences a few weeks ago had taught me that some of these difficult cases became so because of some unfortunate breakdown in the relationship between the Welfare Officer and the person he was trying to help. Here was a case in point:

Jonathan Clarke, a Jamaican, had been resident in England for two years and owned a small, semi-detached house in Brixton where he lived with his wife and ten-year-old son, Bobby, both of whom had joined him in England four months ago. Mr Clarke was employed by British Railways as a guard on goods trains and this meant that he was at work most nights and asleep during the daytime. He was able to give very little attention to his son, who attended a tough neighbourhood school, and gradually the boy took advantage of his mother's easy-going disposition and fell in with a group of little toughs of about his own age. In out-of-school hours these youngsters plagued the local Woolworth store, stealing an assortment of articles which were, for the most part, of little use to themselves, and eventually they were caught and taken to the local police station. Mr Clarke was preparing to go off to his work when a policeman called to tell him of his son's arrest. Feeling angry and humiliated, he went to the police station and heard the tale of his son's pilferings. The boy was bailed into his father's care, with the injunction that he appear at the next sitting of the Juvenile Court.

Mr Clark seemed to meet the situation with remarkable aplomb, but no sooner had he returned home with Bobby than he gave vent to his feelings by thrashing the boy very soundly with a stout leather belt.

Bobby attended school next morning, but at first refused to strip off his shirt and vest for the Physical Training period. When he was finally persuaded to strip, his horrified teacher saw the ugly weals on his body and reported it to his headmaster. The local office of the National Society for the Prevention of Cruelty to Children was promptly informed and the upshot of it was that Bobby was removed to the safety of a Children's Home and Mr Clarke was summoned to appear before the local magistrate. This seemed to him quite intolerable because he felt sure that, as an honest, hard-working and respectable parent it was his right and responsibility to discipline his child without interference from anyone; this was something everyone understood in Jamaica, and he did not either welcome or understand what he considered to be arbitrary intervention in his domestic affairs. He said as much to the magistrate but nevertheless was rather severely reprimanded. Mr Clarke felt hurt and angry. Furthermore, he was told that he would be expected to pay for Bobby's maintenance while the boy remained at the Home, and this seemed to him to be the last straw. He refused. He also refused to attend the hearing of Bobby's case. The Welfare Officer assigned to the case called on Mr Clarke but found him still angry and uncooperative. He refused to see his son, or let his wife see the boy, and further refused to see any official.

This state of affairs had continued for about three months, and then I had been asked to take over. I had discussed the case with my predecessor, then been to see Mr Clarke. There was no reply to my knocking. I wrote him several letters to arrange an interview but without reply. Finally I called at his house one rainy Sunday morning at 9.30 a.m. To do this I had to leave my home in Ilford soon after seven, but I wanted to be sure of catching him soon enough after his night work and before he went to bed, as I knew he would not want to be waked out of his sleep. I pounded his knocker several times before an upstairs window opened and a rather stern-looking Negro shouted at me:

"What the hell do you think you're doing? What do you want?"

"Good morning, are you Mr Clarke?" I asked, looking up at him, the light rain falling on my face.

"Why, what do you want?"

"I've come to see you about Bobby," I replied.

"What about him? Who the hell sent you here at this ungodly hour of the morning?"

"I'm from the Welfare Department, and I've come to discuss the matter with you."

"Oh, so the other one sent you, did he? Well, what I told him goes for you, too. I don't want to talk to any of you and I don't want anybody making a racket at my front door, do you hear? So you clear off back to your white boss and leave me alone."

"I won't take more than a few minutes of your time, Mr Clarke," I promised. "I know you would like to rest yourself, but I'm sure it will help if we have a little talk."

"Okay," he replied, "go on, talk, I can hear you from here, although it won't make any difference. Go on, talk."

Good Lord, I thought, this is going to be tough. How was I going to wangle this?

"Mr Clarke," I said, making my voice less conciliatory, "you really surprise me. You're a West Indian. Since when do West Indians discuss their private business in this way for all and sundry to hear? You must have been away from home a long, long time." I wondered if he'd bite at that. The rain was coming down a little heavier now. This was becoming damned uncomfortable and my neck was feeling a bit stiff.

"All right," he said, at long last. "I'm coming down, but you'd better make it quick."

It took him nearly five minutes to reach the front door. Why should he hurry on my account, I mused; after all, he is cosy and dry inside. My sweet blood-brother.

He opened the door wide enough to stand facing me, but made no move to invite me inside. "Well," he said. I was getting wet and well on the way to losing my temper. After all, Bobby was his son and the least he could do was show me a little courtesy. But if I annoyed him and he shut the door in my face then I'd made the long, tiring journey for nothing.

"Mr Clarke," I said, making it up as I went along, but speaking in a very quiet voice so as to force him to give me his attention. "I think I ought to make my position very clear. I am here at this ungodly hour, as you call it, because I have to be here. In fact, you can call me your servant, as I am paid to serve you in this matter which concerns your son. But I can't serve you if you won't let me. Now you can say to your servant either 'Get the hell away from here' in which case I'll have to go, or 'Okay, come in for a minute and let's talk about it'. Now, I'll do whatever you say to me. What will it be, Mr Clarke?"

He just stood there looking at me, his face showing nothing, not interest, nor anger, nothing. Then, suddenly he smiled; then he laughed and pushing the door wide open he said: "Okay, countryman, come in."

I was relieved. He took me into a warm, comfortable living-room and helped me out of my coat, then we sat down to talk. Or rather he talked. It was a real hate session. He gave me his version of the events and explained his disappointment and humiliation at the discovery that his son was a thief. At this point he became very emotional, very close to tears. So he bashed the boy, but who wouldn't, eh, countryman? When a boy he too had been thrashed for his misdeeds and he was sure it helped him to grow into an honest, God-fearing man. Now these damned interfering people wanted to teach him how to bring up his own son. Well, to hell with them, if they were so sure that they could do a better job, let them get on with it. But they wouldn't get a red cent out of him. They'd have to put him in jail first. And more of the same.

I let him get it all out of his system, or as much of it as would come out. Then I told him how long I had lived in England and of the way in which things were done in the English society. I explained about the N.S.P.C.C., its origin and the important role it played on behalf of children.

"What is worth noticing, Mr Clarke, is that this society took the same interest in the welfare of your son as they would have taken had he been any other person's child. Apart from your own feelings, that is something to consider. It indicates to me that here are people who are concerned with the well-being of children, all children. Is this not what you want for your son, that in this country he will get equal treatment? Let's look at it this way. As citizens, both you and your son are entitled to protection from any threat to life or limb. If someone else had beaten your son in that way, the law would have given your son its protection and punished the other man. The only difference here is that you, and not a stranger, are the person who has been punished."

I let that bit sink in. He had not thought of it in that way; neither had I until now. But he was in a reasonable mood.

Suddenly switching the discussion, he said: "I want the boy back," as if expecting an argument from me.

"Sure, Mr Clarke," I said. "That's why I'm here. We would like to see your son back here where he belongs. By the way, how is his mother taking his absence?"

He lowered his voice to a conspiratorial whisper. "She's been giving me hell; wants me to go and get him."

"Fine, we'll soon get everything straightened out."

"Countryman," he said, "I'm glad we had this talk. If the other Welfare man had explained things like you did, the boy could have been back home long ago."

"That's not quite fair, is it, Mr Clarke?" I said to him. "After all, you yourself admitted that you didn't give him a chance. He, like myself, would like to help you, is paid to help you, but we also need your co-operation."

We chatted a while longer and I left him, assured that now he would co-operate and before long the whole matter would be straightened out. For me, it was another lesson learned in the appreciation of human dignity. If I wanted to be of service to people, very often I must be prepared to serve them on their terms.

As I walked off down the road I reflected on Mr Clarke's attitude. At first he was very rude and impatient. None of this had anything to do with his colour or mine. He believed he had acted in his son's best interests and considered my intrusion unwarranted. There are many people in Britain, English people, who know all about British policy regarding cruelty to children, and who nevertheless would have given their children just as sound a thrashing for a similar offence. What had been needed early in Mr Clarke's case was patience and an understanding of his parental position, together with the assumption that he might be unfamiliar with the law in Britain as applied to children. He and I talked, not because we are both black. The 'countryman' bit came into it only after I was persistently patient. Countryman. He might even now be wondering if I, too, was a Jamaican.

Chapter
Five

WHENEVER POSSIBLE I MADE an opportunity to visit Roddy. At first he would barely acknowledge me, but gradually he began to accept my presence, occasionally inviting my attention to, or comment on, something relating to a game or other activity with which he was occupied; once he took me on a tour of the grounds surrounding the house, and pridefully showed me the chickens and rabbits which were kept as pets. Everything about him was so completely English that I quite forgot about the colour of his skin, and wondered how anyone could fail to love him and want him.

One day, as we strolled in the grounds, he suddenly pointed to a flash of yellow movement and said: "Flutterby."

"Butterfly," I corrected, following the erratic flight of the small Cabbage Yellow.

"Flutterby," he insisted, with a certain positive finality. The action of the little insect seemed fully to support the name he had coined for it.

One day he suddenly turned from his game of 'bus conductors' to ask me: "Do you know my daddy?" His eyes were grave in thought, as if the question was part of a deep longing, not understood, but persistent and disturbing. Probably my answer could be part of the same thing, and for a moment I wished I could work miracles.

"No, Roddy," I replied, "but I wish I did."

"Susan said you're my daddy's friend because you're black."

Abruptly he turned again to his game, as if vaguely conscious that I could offer very little in that direction.

The weeks slipped by without any word from the Rosenbergs or the Welfare Officer who was asked to interview them, and I was getting more and more concerned; then one morning Hardwick rang me. "Rick?"

"Speaking. Oh, hello, Hardwick." I'd recognized his voice, belatedly.

"What's happening?"

"The usual round, you know. No difficulties which a nice little car won't solve."

"Then get one."

"Can't afford it. What can I do for you?"

"You can tell your Welfare people to get a move on about my application. It's over three weeks and no answer from them. You told me they were sending someone to see us from this area. When is he coming, next year? Or have they decided that we are not acceptable as foster-parents?"

I made excuses as quickly as I could think of them, but they may have sounded unconvincing, because I was as irritated as he by the delay; however, I promised to follow the matter myself and let him have some news in a few days. Afterwards I telephoned the

Area office concerned; a Welfare Officer had been assigned to visit the Rosenbergs, but had not yet 'got around to it'.

I spoke with that officer, and explained that there was some urgency about the matter, and finally extracted a promise that she would make the visit before the end of the week.

I remembered the address of Roddy's mother which Miss Storey had given me, and, acting on impulse, decided to have a try at finding her.

The address was in a dingy side street, not far from Paddington Station; the apartment house was, from the outside, as clean as the prevailing soot and grime allowed. Miss Williams' flat was at street level; the closed door and heavily curtained windows gave it a somewhat deserted air, and it was without much hope of finding her in that I knocked on the door. I heard movement inside, then the door was opened. She stood there, blinking in the bright sunshine, her slim figure wrapped around in a thick towel robe, the long, wavy brown hair hanging slackly around her face and on to her shoulders. A pretty face, girlish, except for the eyes, large, brown, regarding me with casual inquiry.

"Well?"

"Good afternoon. Are you Miss Williams?"

"What if I am?"

"I'd like to talk to you."

"What about?"

"Your son Roddy."

"What about him?" The voice was flat, the eyes cool, unwavering, the attitude relaxed, casual, deliberate. I had the feeling that if I made the slightest slip, said the wrong thing, she would just as casually slam the door in my face.

"I'm the Welfare Officer dealing with his case, and I thought it would be nice to meet his mother and have a talk with her."

She stared at me a long moment before replying: "What's there to talk about?"

"Perhaps you'd like to know how he's progressing." Her question had left me floundering in uncertainty.

"No, I wouldn't like to know." No change whatever in expression or voice.

"Couldn't we discuss the matter indoors, Miss Williams?" I felt at a disadvantage standing there. She considered this awhile, then suddenly said: "Okay, come in."

The room I entered was small, clean, and pleasantly furnished, but musty, as if rarely used; she closed a door which probably led into a bedroom, then opened the heavy curtains across the windows, letting sunlight into the room. We sat at opposite ends of a narrow settee. She crossed her legs and wrapped herself carefully in the terry-robe.

"Well?"

"He's a very fine little fellow."

"So?"

"I'm trying to find foster-parents for him, to get him out of the Home."

"Well, what do you want from me?"

Irritation was slowly crowding all the good intentions out of my mind.

"Don't you care anything about him?" I asked her.

"No." The word came out flat and definite. I sat looking at her, wondering about the protracted process which finally made her like this. Something must have been happening inside her also, for now she leaned forward. "Look." A new strident note was in her voice. "I made up my mind before he was born that I would not look at him, wouldn't have anything to do with him. I've never seen him, don't know what he looks like, don't want to know. I've had enough, do you hear, and I'm finished with that."

"Wouldn't you like to see him? He's really a lovely child."

"No, I don't want to see him." She stood up and moved behind the settee, as if wishing to put some protective barrier between us. "He's better off where he is. I didn't want no child in the first place and I told them so. That woman who came to see me a long time ago, I told her. So what do you want to come bothering me again for?"

I thought of something else.

"We've been trying for a long time to locate you."

"I've been away."

"The Council will expect you to make some contribution to the child's upkeep, or if you know where his father is we could try to get in touch with him."

"You and the Council can expect what the hell you like." There was no anger in her voice, only boredom. "I don't know where his father is and I don't want to know. I'm not working, so I've got no money to give them."

I looked around the room; for someone unemployed she seemed to be doing quite well. However, that was none of my business. She must have observed my glance, for now she fairly blazed at me: "Well, what are you looking at?"

I did not answer, but stood up, bade her good-bye and left. It was obvious that she had succeeded in shutting the child completely out of her life, had never allowed herself to know him or care about him, and there seemed to be no point in pursuing it with her. Perhaps, as she had said, Roddy was better off without her. I would report on my interview with her and leave it to those concerned with payments to see her about contributions for the child, but I held no hope for their success.

Hardwick called me a few days later with the news that one of 'my people' had called to see him. I laughed at that because I knew that, this time, 'my people' referred to someone from the Welfare Department; there seemed to be no end to my identity.

He told me that the Welfare Officer, a woman, had asked a multitude of questions about their religion, number of rooms, the flat, the kind of work they did, and things like that, but had showed little interest in the fact that they wanted to give the child a home. Then she had warned them about problems which were likely to occur as the child grew older.

"What sort of problems?" I interrupted.

She had not mentioned anything specific, but broadly hinted at dark doings, so much so that even Hannah lost her patience and said a few rather sharp things.

"Those questions are all part of a pattern she's expected to follow," I explained, "she was not asking them out of personal curiosity." At this he fairly blazed at me, with the retort that if applicants are generally given the impression that some children are suspect and fostering involves a variety of risks, he was not surprised that so many of them remained in the Homes.

"Take it easy." I tried to soothe him.

"No, you take it easy," he replied, and went on to remind me that it was more than a month since they'd completed the application forms, and, so far, all that had happened was that an inexperienced young woman had tried to lecture them on the problems of raising children. He rather suspected that either the child was considered unsuitable for them, or they were unsuitable as parents. In any case he wished we'd hurry up and let them know one way or the other. Then before I could say anything else in reply he yelled that Hannah wanted to speak to me. Her voice held traces of laughter, as if she had been overhearing Hardwick's outburst and was amused by it.

"Hi, Rick."

"Hi, Hannah. I hear the Welfare Officer's visit was not a resounding success."

"Not altogether her fault. Hardwick rather frightened the poor thing. I somehow feel that she was a bit disappointed in us, probably thought us odd for wanting a coloured child. How long will it be before we know whether or not our application is successful?"

"As soon as she sends in her report it will be dealt with."

"Weeks?"

"Oh, no, a few days. I'll try to hurry it up."

"Fine, but I don't entertain much hope."

I saw the officer's report a few days later. I think the appropriate description of it would be 'damning with faint praise.' She spoke about the intellectual atmosphere of the home, and the preoccupation of the principals with their own important activities, guardedly suggesting that they would be able to spare very little time for the boy.

The Chief and I discussed the report, and though I attempted some argument in defence of the Rosenbergs, I had to accept her decision. She put it this way:

"From experience, we have learned to rely on the judgement of our field officers; their usefulness and effectiveness depends on that. From this report it would seem that the Rosenbergs' own child is frequently deprived of her parents' company, although it is clear that there is no shortage of love. But for a complete stranger, the close association with the adoptive parents is the important thing—the love could come later. If we must believe this report, and we have no choice but to believe it, Rodwell's position would in no way be improved by placing him with the Rosenbergs."

"They'll be disappointed."

"That cannot be helped; as a matter of fact it is to be preferred to the disappointment or unhappiness of a helpless small boy, don't you think? I will communicate my decision to them as soon as possible."

That was that. Another door firmly closed. So I had to start again.

The following Sunday I visited my friends, the Kinsmans. This time, I told myself, I'd take a different tack. They'd ask me how the job was going, so we'd talk about that and gradually I'd steer the conversation to fostering; if they showed any interest, well and good; if not . . .

There were several other visitors there when I arrived, all of them involved in greater or lesser degree in the theatre; a television producer and his wife, two actresses and their husbands, an agent, and a young playwright who had recently scored a notable success with her first short play for television. It was a friendly, informal gathering, with topics of conversation varied and interesting while they lasted; I was greatly surprised to discover that one of the actresses, widely known for her portrayal of starry-eyed, dim-witted blondes, was a charming, intelligent, and even brilliant conversationalist.

Eventually conversation got around to current changes within the social structure in Britain, and this in turn led to discussion on the various immigrant groups in the country and their contributions to its social, cultural and economic development. We talked of Jewish contributions to industry, education, the lively and static arts. Someone said: "But all those contributions were made in spite of many proscriptions and prejudices."

From another: "Any community of peoples which indulges in restrictive practices of prejudice and discrimination limits itself and inhibits the rate, depth and extent of its own progress."

"Agreed. Every person in a community has a responsibility to make a positive contribution to its development; but the community itself has an equal responsibility to encourage that contribution and even exploit its development."

"Many people in Britain enjoy all the financial benefits of citizenship without making, or being expected to make, any contribution in any way."

"Some people receive financial benefits without enjoying them, and are literally prevented from making any contribution to the country's welfare; I'm referring to the large number of coloured people now living in Britain. The general opinion is that they are undesirable nuisances and should be discouraged from coming to live among us."

"I don't agree that it is a general attitude; it's not practised in the theatre, for instance."

"The theatre is a special milieu."

"That point about personal contribution to social progress, or whatever it was you said, how could that apply to the coloured immigrants; they come here from Africa, India, Pakistan, the West Indies, etc., where standards of work, education, artistic expression, are all considerably lower than ours . . . "

"How can you compare standards of artistic expression? Whoever the artist is, whether Academician or caveman, his only intention is to capture a fragment of truth, to freeze it as seen and recognized. This we try to do, each in his own way, interlacing a thread into the changing tapestry of life; and the colour of one's skin is no criterion of the colour, texture or durability of the threads contributed."

So it fluctuated, back and forth, coming now to the inevitable question of mixed marriages. They were well in their stride and I had the feeling that they were accustomed to these 'bull sessions' and found it stimulating to probe each other's thoughts and feelings. There might have been Jews among them, if one judged that the very knowledgeable way in which some of them presented the case for or against Jews as a minority group differed from their speculations, notions and theories about Negroes. They treated the subject of mixed marriages as a kind of hobby horse. Each one agreed that a person should be free to marry whom he or she chose, but there immediately followed a whole host of conditions, each of which was defended as reasonable by its champion, and as ardently attacked as illiberal by the detractors.

It seemed to me that, in spite of themselves, the very sound of the words 'Negro' or 'black' immediately set them groping in the darkness of inherited attitudes and conditioned behaviour, with here and there a jubilant cry as each discovered a ray of light which promised an exit. They tried to reason themselves into liberal thinking and though I sympathized with their efforts, I wondered how well such reasoning would stand up to some of the tests I encountered day by day. If it were possible I would like to buy up every liberal thought expressed so freely and save it for redistribution in some areas of England; brotherly love was always at a premium, and the more the obvious differences between the brothers the less the loving. Could they reason themselves into liberal action?

I tried to stay on the outer edge of these discussions, hearing, feeling, remembering, recording it all in my mind, or as much as was possible; now and then a question would be put to me and I'd be compelled to say my piece. As when someone suggested that, in mixed marriages, the children were the chief sufferers as they could find no place in either camp, so to speak. To this I replied:

"We seem to be ignoring one important factor. Irrespective of who his parents are, a child born into a family is part of that family, so he naturally belongs, and needs from them love, companionship, help, guidance, encouragement, advice, and example in positive living. He needs these things irrespective of his parents' racial origins. If he is born into a community where tolerance prevails, then there is no special problem. However, a coloured child born in Britain, for instance, not only needs the things I have mentioned, but is severely handicapped without them, because the community considers his colour a handicap and therefore imposes special pressure and proscriptions upon him. He needs those things not as insulation against the pressures, but as sources from which to draw strength in order to meet and deal with them with wisdom, courage and resolution."

"And supposing, for argument's sake, such a child didn't have parents to comfort or advise? Then he is a sitting duck for everything the community feels like throwing at him."

"Community is a blanket word like 'nation' or 'club'; we can so easily wrap ourselves in it and become anonymous. It must be remembered that we contribute to those prejudices as much by not protesting against them as by deliberately acting in agreement."

"But what can one do in matters such as this?"

This was the question I had been hoping to hear; the tailor-made opportunity for me to talk about the increasing number of unwanted children, white and black, in the Council's Homes. I tried hard to be objective about the things I said, merely stating the case without attempting any emphasis, and as soon as I had dealt with the main points and answered their questions, I changed the subject; if anyone wanted to follow it up, they'd have time enough to discuss it further.

Later that afternoon someone started on it; by this time we were all on a Christian-name relationship. So now discussion centred around various suggestions for reducing the numbers of orphan or neglected children in the care of Councils. Someone proposed that an experienced publicity manager be employed to present the case to the public, arguing that there must be thousands of women in Britain who either could not have children or had lost those they had, and in whom the milk of mother-love flowed free and strong. They would jump at the chance of adopting or fostering a child, especially if it were made to seem attractive to them. I said that Councils advertised, rather discreetly and not very much, but they advertised.

Then we got around to discussing the relative merits of fostering 'for pay or for love', as someone put it, and the arguments which followed were very lively. These were experts in the matter of buying or selling ideas which either dictated or catered to public taste and appeal and I listened to them with respect and a certain envy. One of them, the playwright, Olga Keriham suggested: "Why don't they advertise for foster-parents to undertake the care of a child as a job, a paid job, something a sensible, decent housewife could do instead of working all day in a factory, and pay her factory rates or something near it?"

Before I could say anything, someone else replied: "I suppose they don't want the lovely altruism to be dirtied by any mention of filthy lucre. It's a bit like the teaching profession, not quite the thing to expect to be paid for assisting in so worthy a cause."

"Or perhaps they assume that by paying for the job too many undesirable types might be attracted, purely for the money."

"Not necessarily. I'm sure they have some means of investigating each applicant. I think it would be easier and more practicable to assess a person's ability and suitability to do a job of work, for pay, than for any other motive, no matter how laudable it seemed."

They had completely taken over the discussion, and I was pleased to be there, just listening.

"If it were made a paid job, it would be none the less worthwhile. Besides, it would encourage many more people to foster the handicapped children."

"Including the black ones?"

"Including the black ones. Funny, but when people are doing a job for money, that can be the best excuse for doing the job, it can also give the job respectability. As it is I am sure that many a British housewife would not now offer a home to a coloured child through fear of being suspected of certain emotional motives, whereas as a job, she could undertake it with less concern for the opinions of others."

"I've just thought of something," Olga said, "instead of waiting for a few high-minded people to come forward, they should not only pay foster-parents a practical wage, but also run short courses for them so that they have an opportunity to learn how to cope with such problems as might arise. I believe that if several persons are engaged in a similar activity, it helps them if they meet others similarly occupied, for exchanging ideas and general discussion, and for the security which comes from knowing that you are not some kind of freak doing something unusual."

"That would provide more foster-parents without discouraging the altruistic ones."

"Why, certainly."

"Wouldn't the home atmosphere be rather sterile if people were merely concerned with fostering as a job of work?"

"Hell, no. Put an adult and a child together and you go a long way to having a family. If the adult begins by caring for the child's needs and wants in health and sickness, some relationship is bound to develop between them. I'm sure that such relationships develop even in the Homes Ricky spoke about, where one housemother is expected to divide her attention, care and even love, between several children."

"And what about the children? How would you know that they are receiving good value for the money paid?"

"By the same system of supervision now in operation."

It all seemed so very reasonable and practical that I immediately suspected there would be many snags not readily noticeable. If an impromptu discussion could produce such pertinent opinions, it seemed reasonable to assume that similar ideas must have occurred to those in authority within the Welfare Department, and if no action had yet been taken on any of the lines suggested, it might well be that there were excellent reasons for it.

However, the ideas so simply stated invited action. I thought about them. They tossed ideas back and forth, sometimes drawing me in with a question but answering it themselves before I could attempt a reply. Very interesting and entertaining, even, but I felt that they would just as engagingly have discussed any other subject, from their safe position outside, uninvolved. But, perhaps not all of them.

As the party broke up Olga Keriham offered me a lift in her car, and, on the way surprised me with: "When you speak of foster-parents, Ricky, is it always necessary that there be two of them? Could not a person, a man or a woman, apply to foster a child? What I mean is, is your department only interested in two married people?"

I took a long look at her. Her eyes were large, clear grey, and steady; her face lean, tight-skinned and shiny smooth with a combination of careful make-up and good health. She wore her pale blonde hair in a high plaited chignon which emphasized the small shapely chin and slim neck. About thirty years old, I thought; without effort she'll keep that figure for a long time.

"Well?" she prompted.

"There maybe exceptions," I replied, "but generally applications are considered from couples, so that the fostered child can enter into a normal family situation."

"But supposing a person, a single person, happened to have the financial means and interest to consider fostering a child?"

"I couldn't answer that one without checking my authority. I suppose there may be special circumstances."

"I'd like to get to know one of those children, a coloured one," she remarked. It was more like an incomplete thought being tested for sound than a question directed at me.

"Could do." I was soon telling her about Roddy and my abortive attempts, so far, to find him a home.

"Poor woman."

"She's okay," I said. "Roddy is the one who needs the sympathy."

"Perhaps, but why did she go to the trouble of having the child? I don't suppose that a man could understand about that. Do you suppose they'd let a complete stranger see the boy? Just for a visit?"

"Like who?"

"Like me."

I assured her that it could be arranged and promised to ring her as soon as I had discussed it with the Matron.

Two days later Olga and I went to see Roddy. From the wide window of Matron's office we could see the children playing together on the rough lawn behind the building, singing at the tops of their voices as they held hands in a revolving circle. Roddy was the only coloured child in the group. I offered to take her out and make the introduction, but she demurred, her eyes on Matron in unspoken question. Matron nodded, understanding that something.

I watched from the window as she reached the group, hesitated awhile as the action slowed, then intervened between Roddy and his neighbour. So accustomed were the children to new faces and situations in their small world, that the game continued with hardly a pause. Later, when they tired of it and broke up into their separate interests, I saw Roddy leading her away on what I was sure would be a tour of the house and grounds.

Matron and I talked about Olga, and I mentioned her expressed willingness to foster a child. As I had guessed, there was not much chance that the Council would accept an application from a single person, but Matron suggested that Olga might like to become an Official Auntie. That would make it possible for her to visit him, take him out for short periods, and, if no foster-parents appeared for him, she might later be allowed to have him spend the odd day or weekend with her. I felt sure Olga would like that.

"About the other, any luck?" Matron asked. I knew she was referring to my search for foster-parents.

"Not yet, but one presses on regardless," I replied.

"Time's slipping by."

I didn't need to be reminded. The thought of his being moved to another Home for older children depressed me, try as I might to keep the plain realities in perspective. This place was Roddy's little world, in which he was safe and loved; unless foster-parents were found for him, and soon, he'd have to leave it and start again, from scratch, probably with an overworked housemother, and in new and unfamiliar surroundings. So far I had exhausted my first line of contacts and I did not quite know how to proceed from there. I was often invited to address groups of people in and around London and endeavoured, whenever the opportunity presented itself, to mention the plight of the increasing number of children in the care of local councils, hoping to stimulate some interest in fostering or adoption, but so far nothing significant had developed.

When the break came it was completely unexpected. I was alone in my office one afternoon when the phone rang; the switchboard operator asked me if I would take an emergency call from a local hospital as the duty officer was busy with interviews and no other Welfare Officer was in the building. I accepted the call and spoke with the hospital's almoner. She told me that a young West Indian woman had that morning been admitted to hospital as an ambulance case—premature delivery. The woman's other children, twin girls, were in the rooms she occupied, uncared for except for a neighbour's promise to 'look in' on them. I assured her that the matter would be attended to without delay. It sounded very efficient and grand when I said it, but soon after replacing the telephone on its hook I realized that I hadn't a single clue about what to do in such a situation. I went downstairs to get some help from Miss Martindale, the duty officer, but she was deep in an interview with two women, apparently a mother and daughter. I walked over to the telephonist's cubicle. As usual, Miss Felden beat me to it.

"That you, Mr Braithwaite?"

"Yes, this is me."

"You sound bothered. What's the trouble?"

"A call just came in from the Almoner at St Saviour's. A woman has been rushed off to hospital and her two little twin children are to be taken into care, but I don't know the drill."

"That's simple," she laughed, and told me what to do. First I had to see Mrs Bereton in the Administration Section; she would shop around all the Children's Residential Nurseries for vacancies. The vacancies might be any place—London, Kent, Essex. It was a pity I hadn't a car.

"One thing more," Miss Felden said. "You have to get the children to a clinic and have them examined and passed fit before the Home will accept them, so I think you should let Mrs Bereton know the woman's address and she'll tell you which is the nearest clinic in that area."

I thanked her and went along the corridor to Mrs Bereton's office; tall, blonde and efficient, she consulted a list of children's Residential Nurseries, made some telephone calls, and finally said: "Not bad, not good. The only place I could find two vacancies is at Brighton, nothing nearer."

"It will have to do," I said.

"How will you get them there?"

"By train, I expect."

"Good. I've told them to expect you."

Once again I sought Miss Felden's help. She telephoned Victoria Station for information on trains to Brighton. There was a fast train soon after four o'clock. It was now nearly two o'clock, which gave me about two hours to collect the children, have them examined and make the train.

Outside the office I called a taxi and gave the children's address; it proved to be in a narrow sidestreet near Kennington Park Road, Newington. An old, ramshackle house in a dismal terrace. The street door was open, so I asked the taxi to wait and walked into a gloomy, untidy corridor. I knocked on the nearest door but nobody answered. From the floor above I heard sounds and went up the stairs, listened to locate them and knocked on the door behind which I heard movement.

A Negro woman opened it just wide enough to let me see part of her face, hardly discernible against the room's gloomy interior.

"Who is it?"

"I'm from the Welfare Office," I told her. "A woman from this building was taken to hospital this morning, and I'm here to collect her two children."

She opened the door a little wider, the better to examine me, it seemed.

"They're in the room downstairs," she said. "I told her I'd keep an eye on them, but I've been very busy."

"Which room?"

"The first door at the bottom of the stairs." The door was closing before I turned and hurried down.

The room was small, overcrowded with the double bed, plain table, straight-backed chair and children's cot. At least it seemed overcrowded, perhaps because of the general disorder. The large bed was covered with a mess of rumpled blankets and sheets, soiled towels and a heterogeny of articles of clothing. On the table were dirty dishes and cooking utensils. The narrow cot near the bed seemed cluttered up with hastily discarded garments, and I nearly missed the children. They were lying together, nearly hidden by the tumbled coverlets, absolutely quiet, the four bright eyes observing me in the gloom with an expression which seemed to be a mixture of fear and resignation, terrible to see in their tiny faces.

I switched on the light and leaned over the cot, about which hung the heavy aroma of urine. I removed the coverlet. The twins were lying close together, their nappies saturated from the urine which remained in a shallow pool on the waterproof rubberized covering stretched over the cot's thin mattress. They could have been no more than a year old, and lay so quiet beneath my intrusive gaze that I guessed they must have long ago exhausted themselves of tears. I cannot remember another instance of such utter human helplessness. It was now soon after two o'clock, these children had lain there unattended all morning, dirty, hungry and very frightened. That damned woman upstairs had not bothered even to change their wet nappies. I couldn't take them like that to the clinic. I rushed back up the stairs and hammered on her door.

"Who is it?" Her reply sounded hollow behind the door.

"The Welfare Officer."

Again she opened the door only wide enough to see me.

"The children downstairs need to be washed and changed before I can take them away. Will you help me with them?"

"I can't come down. I've got my own children to attend to." Even as she spoke the door was being closed, and she quickly turned the key in the lock as if afraid that I would grab her and drag her forcibly out.

I remembered the taxi-driver was still waiting outside and rushed out to let him know I'd be delayed for some little time. Suddenly it occurred to me that he might help, so I said:

"I've run into a bit of bother inside. I've come to take a couple of tiny children away to a children's home, and they're inside wet and dirty. Somehow I've got to clean them up."

He tilted his cap away from his forehead.

"What about their mother? Can't she fix them up?"

"They took her off to hospital early this morning."

"Who's in there with them?"

"Nobody."

Without another word he left his taxi and went indoors with me. When he saw the two little black faces regarding him from wide eyes, he exclaimed:

"Poor little buggers. Cor! don't they pong!"

Quickly he set about examining the room. Under the mattress of the double bed we found dry nappies sandwiched between newspapers, and in an old suitcase under the bed were several changes of baby clothes, clean and neatly pressed. He also pulled a large enamelled basin from under the bed. I had been standing rather helplessly by while he assumed command with the familiarity of having done that sort of thing many times before.

"Come on, mate, give us a hand," he called to me.

"What can I do?"

"Get us some hot water, for a start."

I now noticed there was a small gas ring in one corner. I lit it. I found a kettle and filled it from a water tap at the end of the passage and set it on the ring, then filled the enamelled basin half-full from the tap.

My companion had let down one side of the cot and was stripping away the napkin from one infant, murmuring to it meanwhile.

"Cor, talk about sweet violets! Hey, mate," to me, "spread some of that newspaper on the floor to catch this stuff. We'll have to dump it."

When both infants had been stripped he dropped the filthy garments on to the newspapers and I rolled them into a tight bundle and put it into the garbage bin outside the back door. By now the kettle was boiling and I poured the hot water into the basin. He stuck a little finger in to test the temperature, then put both the children into it. I found him a piece of soap and stood aside in admiration of his gentleness and efficiency. As each child was bathed, I dried it on one of the clean napkins, then laid it on the bed for his attention. He was very expert in folding the squares into triangles and fitting them on to the tiny bodies with safety pins; in a short while the children were clean and warmly dressed.

"Who's going to clean this lot up?" he asked, nodding his head towards the unmade bed, the cot and the room in general. When I told him I hadn't a minute to spare, he placed the children in my arms, tossed all the stuff off the bed and soon had it neatly remade; he took the mattress from the cot and draped it over the side, to air, as he explained, emptied the basin and replaced it, together with the suitcase, under the bed. In a few minutes the room was orderly; he switched off the lights and we went out to the taxi.

On the short drive to the clinic near Kennington Park Road I sat with the children cradled in my arms, but my thoughts were on the driver, this short, compact, red-necked man who had, in the past few moments, exhibited such kindliness and humanity that I was filled with wonder at it. More touching than his knowledgeable care of the children was his concern for the unknown woman, that she should not return to a dirty, disordered room. He had said it wouldn't take a minute, when there was every justification for leaving it as it was.

When we arrived at the clinic, he helped me indoors with the infants who had, as yet, uttered not the least sound. I explained my business and need for haste to the Matron in charge, and the children were immediately examined, declared free from infection, and issued with a certificate to be handed over to the residential nursery.

I believe that my friend the taxi driver broke a few traffic regulations on our way to Victoria Station. Arrived there, he helped me by taking care of the children while I purchased my ticket. When I paid him I expressed my thanks but he waved that aside with the remark:

"I've kids of my own, mate. In this world, you never know when you'll need a helping hand."

I suppose I must have presented a curious sight as I rushed for my train with an infant clutched tightly under each arm. Once aboard, I laid them down side by side on the wide seat of a compartment and sat beside them. Just then I realized that the poor things had not been fed all day, but there was nothing I could now do about it; as soon as we arrived at the nursery I'd tell the person in charge about it.

Just before the train started a young woman took the seat opposite us. Probably about thirty years old, with a pleasant open face and short brown hair prematurely grey-streaked. She looked at the children, then at me, and favoured us with a friendly smile.

"Twins?" she asked.

"Yes." They were identical except for a narrow silver bracelet which one wore on a dimpled wrist; I suppose the mother's attempt at identification.

"Boy and girl?"

"No, both girls."

"Your wife not with you?"

I guessed she thought they were mine.

"Their mother is in hospital. I have no idea where their father is. I'm taking them to a nursery at Brighton."

She fixed me with her large grey eyes as if trying to sort out the meaning of my remark.

"I'm a Welfare Officer," I explained.

From this we fell into some discussion of children in residential homes, and I spoke of the difficulties experienced in trying to find foster-parents, especially for the coloured children. As I spoke I observed how her face mirrored an interesting interplay of surprise and disbelief. I suppose I even laid it on a bit thick, stressing that a black skin was considered their greatest disability.

"What nonsense," she exclaimed. She sounded rather like my mother when in disagreement with something or other. I thought, how easy it is to say 'nonsense' about circumstances in which she would perhaps never be involved; I'd met the type before. They'd severely censure others for action which they themselves would never undertake, cavorting comfortably behind a façade of self-righteous indignation. I immediately had the crazy idea to put it to her.

"Would you be prepared to foster a black child?" I asked.

"Why, of course." Her reply was immediate, without the slightest hesitation, and, it seemed to me, without the least thought. After all, what chance was there that her expressed liberality would be put to the test? Oh Hell, let's stop kidding ourselves. I suddenly decided that there was nothing to be gained by pursuing the conversation, and turned my attention to the darkening pastoral scenes which flitted by.

"Don't you believe me?" Somehow it sounded more like an accusation than a question. "If we could afford it I'd take one tomorrow, and I'm sure my husband would have no objections at all."

Well, there it was. The 'if we could afford it' sealed the matter firmly and finally. These people always left themselves a neat escape clause, just in case. Okay, I thought, let's forget it and talk about something else.

"Any children of your own?" I asked.

"Two. Girls. Six and eight. Both at school. My husband's taking care of them tonight while I run up to Brighton to visit his mother. She's been ailing somewhat and we take turns to visit when we can."

"Do you live in London?'

"No, Middlesex. My husband works in London."

During this pleasant exchange a half-formed idea was nagging my mind, and now it suddenly popped into my mouth before I had time to examine it.

"You said you and your husband would consider fostering children if you could afford it. What exactly did you mean by 'afford it'?"

"If we had enough money to do it. We have everything else. A comfortable home, big enough to accommodate one or two more children, and I'm at home all day long."

It had fallen into my lap like a ripe apple. After weeks of searching, watching the time slip away without any hope of a positive lead, this had happened. Then came the sobering thought that by my churlishness I might have messed it up; but my companion did not seem to hold that against me, and we were soon in earnest conversation about herself, her home and family as they might favourably or otherwise affect the possibility of fostering a child.

I learned that she did part-time work for a typing agency, and a local newspaper; the work was varied and interesting, but important mainly in that it provided some very necessary extra money. As she spoke memory came flooding back about the discussions at Reena's house. Maybe here was a possible break for Roddy, and perhaps a chance to try out an idea or two. But slow and easy. Remembering my previous failures I'd go very slowly on this one, slow and easy.

"Foster-parents are paid," I said. "Not much, but they're paid."

"Well, then, there's no problem," she replied. "Instead of doing part-time work I could take care of a child or two. I'd like to, if I received about the same for doing it as I make from part-time work."

My excitement had really taken hold, though I was trying very hard to keep it out of my voice and face. To keep things sort of impersonal I asked what kind of children she would be willing to foster.

"Do you mean what age? Not too young, I'd say. A new set of nappies suddenly appearing on the line would certainly set the neighbours chattering. Or perhaps you mean would we have a coloured one? What difference does it make?" I let that pass and asked if she had any special preference for boys or girls.

"Doesn't really matter, but my girls might prefer to have brother; too many women in the family already."

We chatted around and I asked if I might come up to their home, on my return, to meet her husband and children and discuss the matter further after she'd had some time to think it over.

"Good. I'm returning home tomorrow. Could you come up in the evening? It's the only time you'd be able to see us together."

"That's a date."

"Have you some children in mind?"

"One in particular, at the moment," I replied, and, acting on impulse, I told her about Roddy.

"Sounds a lovely chap," she said, "I'm sure John will agree to having him. That's my husband."

At this point we introduced ourselves and she gave me her address near Wealdstone in Middlesex.

The twins slept throughout the ride. It struck me as odd that not once had either of them made any sound, from the moment I walked into the room in Kennington until now. The fears I had half-entertained of squalling infants were, happily, unfulfilled.

At Brighton, Mrs Tamerlane, my travelling companion, helped me with the children, and I quickly found a taxi to take me to the Nursery. I think the Matron was rather surprised that I, a man, had undertaken to bring the twins all the way from London. I mentioned that I thought they had not been fed all day, and left them with her, relieved by the knowledge that they were in good, capable hands.

Next morning I went to St Saviour's Hospital to see Miss Bruce, the mother of the twins. She looked tired, but cheered up appreciably when I told her that the girls were safe at a residential nursery on the south coast where they would be well cared for until she was able to have them home again.

"What is it this time?" I asked.

"A boy." She seemed absurdly young, eighteen or nineteen I guessed. "Were they all right—in the room, I mean?" she asked.

"They were fine."

"I must remember to thank Mrs Sawyer when I go home."

Thank her very much for nothing, I thought, and let it go at that. No point in telling her about the state in which I found the children.

"By the way, Miss Bruce, would you tell me where I can get in touch with the twins' father? We'll have to inform him that the children have been taken into care, as he will be expected to make some contribution to their maintenance."

"I don't know where he is," she replied, "he stopped coming to see me when I told him I was pregnant again. I went around to where he lived in Brixton, but they told me he'd moved away, gone up North somewhere. He hasn't written me or anything." As she spoke the tears slipped in a steady stream down the side of her face.

"So how have you been making out?"

"The people from Dr Barnardo's have been helping me. They send me some money each week. And the Moral Welfare people too, but they say I must take out a summons against him for maintenance. But how can I? I don't know where he is."

God, what a mess. Three young children and nothing to hold on to.

"I don't know if the landlord will let me have the room when I leave here. He used to fuss about me having the twins in the room. Said he didn't want children in the place. So I know what he'll say about the baby. Then there's the rent."

A passing nurse noticed the tears and came over to her.

"Now, now, Miss Bruce, what's this? Crying again? Now, we don't want to upset ourselves, do we?" Then to me, "Something wrong?"

"She's worried about her room at Kennington," I said.

"Now, now, not to worry," she comforted her. "I'll ask the Almoner to come up and discuss it with her later on. She'll know what to do."

I left soon afterwards. In my report, I'd recommend that the twins remain at the nursery as long as possible after Miss Bruce left hospital, to give her an opportunity to sort things out, probably with the help of one of the voluntary organizations with which she was already in touch. On the way out I chatted briefly with the Almoner and learned that Miss Bruce had arrived in England from

Jamaica eighteen months ago. Probably the need for companionship in a strange country had precipitated this chain of unfortunate events; now, with three small children and herself to support, the future seemed bleak indeed.

"She's a charming, attractive girl," the Almoner said, "but rather soft, I should imagine. I hope the next man to come along will stick by her."

That evening I went to see the Tamerlanes. Theirs was a semi-detached, two-storeyed house in a pleasant tree-lined street a short distance from the centre of town. When he opened the door, Mr Tamerlane tried to welcome me and at the same time restrain a large, shaggy dog which seemed bent on reaching up to lick my face. Standing behind him were his wife and two chubby, fair-haired girls who looked startlingly alike, although one was somewhat taller than the other. They came forward to shake hands and immediately unleashed a barrage of questions about the new "brother Mummy had said would be coming to stay with them".

From the very first moment there was no pretence at formality, and I thought it would be a wonderful thing if Roddy were introduced into this easy, friendly atmosphere. Apparently Mrs Tamerlane had already discussed the matter with her family. My first reaction was quick annoyance that she had jumped the gun, but I soon realized that this family operated as a unit, and anything as important as an addition to it would require general discussion, especially as the girls would eventually be the ones upon whom the success or failure of the matter would depend.

The family had just finished their evening meal, but I was

invited to share a cup of tea with them. Jacqueline, the elder of the two girls, asked me:

"What's your name?"

"Ricky Braithwaite."

"Uncle Ricky, is he like you, our new brother?"

"Not quite, but near enough, I suppose." The question had caught me off balance.

"What's his name?"

"Roddy. Roddy Williams."

"How old is he?"

"Just five, I think."

"Then he'll go to the Infants' like Junie." I later learned that the schools the girls attended consisted of a single building for the Infants' and Junior sections.

"Oh goody, goody," from Junie. "Can we go to see him?"

"I suppose so, as soon as it can be arranged."

Mrs Tamerlane intervened and suggested that the girls go and play with their dolls and let the grown-ups have an opportunity to talk in peace; they complied immediately, but I noticed that they brought their dolls to a spot well within earshot of us. Mr Tamerlane set the ball rolling.

"Ella has told me of the conversation she had with you while travelling to Brighton, and I gather that she has more or less committed us to fostering one of your youngsters."

"We chatted in very general terms, Mr Tamerlane; I don't think she committed you in any way."

"Maybe so, but she is very enthusiastic about it, and as you may have noticed," he slanted his head towards his daughters, "she's thoroughly infected the rest of us."

"However, she and I have discussed it together; as you can see, we have quite enough room—I'll show you over the house before you leave—so there would be no problem about accommodation. The only difficulty which could arise would be financial. If it were possible, we'd be happy to have the boy in our family without any thought of assistance from your Council, but in our present circumstances, that isn't possible. Again, we think it would be unfair to June and Jackie to take on anything which would mean their having to do without the few amenities they now have. If the boy joins our family, we'd like to continue in the same way, with him as an additional member, no less. Ella and I are in agreement that in the child's interests it would be necessary for her to give up her part-time work, in order to give him as much attention as possible, especially during the first months when he's likely to find family life very strange, and school a new and disturbing experience."

"One thing you did not mention, darling," his wife interrupted, "we also agreed that it would be a good thing to have another man around the house; this one is becoming terribly spoiled with three women fussing over him, and anyway, it would be fine for the girls to have a brother to take care of."

"Did you have any definite figure in mind?"

Mrs Tamerlane told me how much she earned from her part-time job. I thought of what it cost the Council each week to maintain a child in one of its Homes or Nurseries, and suggested that she consider a figure somewhat in excess of the amount she mentioned, but considerably less than the weekly *per capita* cost to the Council; the small overlap would prove useful in view of the 'extra mouth'.

That settled, I was shown over the house, with the whole

family and the dog in attendance. On the upper floor were separate bathroom and toilet facilities, and three bedrooms; a small ante-room or box-room was sandwiched between two of the bedrooms. They were all comfortably furnished; the girls each occupied a bedroom.

"I think it would be best for him to share Junie's bedroom," Mrs Tamerlane said. "It's big enough for two beds, and with someone near he'd settle down more easily; we could always make other arrangements later on."

This started June and Jacqueline off on an excited discussion of how best to rearrange June's room, and they remained behind when we continued downstairs. On the lower floor was a large sitting-room, dining-room and spacious kitchen, from which a door led out to a pleasant grassy backyard, dominated by a patient looking oak-tree, which showed signs of having been well climbed. From its lowest limb two slim chains supported a swing seat. A thick privet hedge separated this backyard from a stretch of common meadow, and I noticed in one or two places the unmistakable signs that a small body could gain easy access to and from the meadow.

The more I saw of this home and its occupants, the more it seemed the right place for Roddy, and I resolved to spare no effort to bring them together. I promised to keep in close touch with the Tamerlanes; I'd arrange for them to visit Roddy as soon as I had cleared the lines with my Chief.

Next morning I made an appointment with her, and prepared a short résumé of my meeting with Mrs Tamerlane and my visit to her home. I realized I had been precipitate in making an offer for maintenance to the Tamerlanes which was much larger than that usually paid to foster-parents, but argued with myself that the special circumstances dictated special measures and hoped that the Supervisor would take the same view, although as the time for our meeting approached the likelihood of her agreement dwindled.

In her office I gave her the facts briefly and clearly; upon reflection it seems to me that I stated them somewhat aggressively, probably in anticipation of a fight with her over the financial issues involved. She seemed to take an unreasonably long time before replying, then, "I think we'll have quite a fight on our hands."

There was more than the hint of a smile around her mouth, and I had the feeling that she knew I expected a refusal.

"This sounds like a nice family," she continued, "but now we have the problem of it's being located in foreign territory, so to speak. County Councils do not take a very favourable view of others who poach on their preserves, and foster-parents are in such short supply that Middlesex may well feel they have prior claim to the Tamerlanes. However, that is not our main problem. The maintenance figure you suggest is several times greater than that generally paid to foster-parents, either by us or by Middlesex, and that may well prove to be our most difficult hurdle. We cannot simply barge into another Council's territory and dispense maintenance grants more attractive than theirs. Rightly or wrongly, we would lay ourselves open to all kinds of criticism and, furthermore, run the grave risk of disrupting the very useful co-operation which exists. If word got around, and it very likely would, that a certain family was receiving special maintenance rates, other foster-parents might consider themselves similarly entitled, and with justification. So, you see, we are on what might be called a very sticky wicket."

There was no arguing with her clear reasonableness; as I listened, my enthusiasm was slipping lower and lower, and I could see another door slowly closing. It was also becoming increasingly clear that there was a great deal I had to learn about this business. She must have observed the dismay reflected in my face, for she said:

"However, let's not lose heart before we begin. Our best plan is to proceed normally and deal with each issue as it arises. Get the Tamerlanes to make formal application as foster-parents, and attach your recommendation for special maintenance. Naturally, before I endorse it, either Miss Whitney or I will have to pay a visit to the Tamerlanes."

Remembering what happened with the Rosenbergs, I said:

"I'd like to follow through with this case."

"Of course," she replied.

"One other thing. From what you have said of the difficulties we may run into, could it be arranged that Roddy remain where he is for the time being? He is due to be transferred to a children's home in a week or two; and that would present a further problem especially if he is sent off some distance from London."

"I think that's reasonable, I'll have a word with the Matron, but I'd prefer that you make no attempt to introduce the Tamerlanes to the boy until after I've seen them."

Immediately after leaving her office I sent the application forms to John and Ella Tamerlane, then telephoned the Matron at Roddy's nursery to bring her up to date on the situation; I knew that in her I had a very strong ally.

"What about your friend?" she asked. I guessed she meant Olga.

"She's fine, I expect she'll be coming out there now and then, whenever she can. Lucky for her she has a car. She's tickled at the idea of being someone's aunt, next best thing to being someone's mother, I suppose."

"She made a conquest here. Roddy's done nothing but talk about her since she left."

"What?" I said, in mock alarm, "no mention of me?"

"You're a mere man," she replied.

The Chief called me to her office two days later.

"Sorry I could not get out to see the Tamerlanes personally," she said, "but Miss Whitney paid them a visit and strongly recommends them; she's brought the completed forms, so I think it will be in order for them to visit the boy. However, I would suggest that you move slowly and carefully, because I rather suspect that this matter will take some considerable time before it is finally resolved. That being so, it may be necessary for us to take some action in respect of the boy's entry into school, as that cannot be postponed indefinitely, but we can safely leave that hurdle until we come to it. Incidentally, I've just been speaking with the Matron at the nursery; seems that Rodwell has acquired a new aunt. Never rains but it pours, wouldn't you say?"

I couldn't be certain, but it seemed there was a twinkle in her eye as she said this.

That afternoon I telephoned Matron and arranged for the Tamerlanes to visit Roddy; she suggested Saturday afternoon as the best time for a first visit as that was the time most parents appeared. Then I rang Mrs Tamerlane and passed on the news. I suggested that she and her husband should first make the trip, alone, but here I found her suddenly stubborn, insisting that the girls were on tenterhooks to meet Roddy, and "after all the whole family is concerned in this". I gave in.

Now that we seemed to be making some headway with this case I had a feeling of guilt about the way I had been neglecting the others; anyway, there was nothing further I could do until the Chief had had discussions with the Middlesex authorities, and, for the time being, with Olga and the Tamerlanes in the picture, Roddy was well catered for.

Chapter
Six

THE NEXT CASE I tackled concerned a girl, Brigid Sweeney, whose daughter, Patricia, aged three years, was in a residential nursery. According to the previous Welfare Officer's report, Patricia had been taken into the Council's care because, following the birth, her mother was without fixed residence and unemployed. Miss Sweeney was now working as a waitress at one of a well-known group of self-service restaurants, but resisted all efforts at encouragement to have her baby with her, although she visited the child regularly, at least once a week. Patricia's father, a West Indian from Barbados, also visited the child, but separately from Miss Sweeney, taking her 'extravagantly expensive gifts' from time to time, although he made no contribution to the child's maintenance. The Welfare Officer had not been able to have any discussion with him, because Miss Sweeney 'either did not know or refused to divulge' his address or any other information about him. No mention was made of either parent's age.

Miss Sweeney lived in a rooming house near Clerkenwell Green. I called there about five o'clock in the evening. There were no name plates of the occupants, so I pressed the only push button. After some delay an elderly woman opened the door. Big face and neck, short-sleeved and shapeless overcoat, a yellow headkerchief kept tightly curled hair firmly in place.

She opened the door and stood there completely filling the doorway, regarding me through pale grey eyes which seemed grim and staring, probably because of the thin fringe of pale blonde eyelashes.

"Who do you want?" There was no mistaking that lilt in her voice. Irish, without a doubt.

"I'm looking for Miss Sweeney."

"What do you want with her?"

My immediate reaction to the clear hostility of her attitude and tone was to ask her very rudely, 'What business is it of yours?' But I did not know if she was the young woman's friend, relative or neighbour, and with an effort I kept my temper controlled.

"I'd like to see her on an important personal matter," I said.

"Like what?"

"I'm afraid I'm not at liberty to discuss that with you. Is Miss Sweeney in?"

"No."

"Any idea when I might find her in?"

"Did that Mr Man send you here?"

"What Mr Man?"

"Him as used to come here; a feller like yourself."

"I don't know whom you mean. I'm here to see Miss Sweeney on official business."

She stared at me through those eyes which seemed disturbingly transparent and lifeless, and finally said: "You wait a minute." She left the door open, turned and walked down a narrow passage-way, moving her bulk lightly and gracefully, now I noticed that she wore small, high-heeled mules which seemed surprisingly out of character. After about five minutes she reappeared, accompanied by a somewhat younger edition of herself; the same broad face and thick, wide-hipped body. This one had about her a certain attraction, an animal ripeness, full-bosomed, pink-cheeked, wide mouthed, strong.

The younger one came to the door and examined me with a cool, comprehensive sweep of her eyes. "Who are you from?" she asked.

"Are you Miss Sweeney?"

"Yes."

In my mind I had conjured up a picture of a young, inexperienced, rather helpless person. This woman was, I felt sure, at least on the shady side of thirty.

"I'm from the Welfare Department."

"Oh,"—she did not smile, but her face became relaxed. Perhaps she, too, had thought I was on some other errand.

"Won't you come in?" I followed where she led along the passage. The other woman had remained standing nearby, within easy earshot; now she drew herself nearer to let us pass, still fixing me with those hostile eyes.

Miss Sweeney led me into her room, small but well-kept. At her invitation, I sat down in a high-backed chair, while she sat on a settee. She was composed and friendly.

"For a moment I was afraid your friend would prove difficult," I said—anything for an opening line.

"She's my sister. After my trouble I came to live with her. Have you come about Pat?"

"Yes. The Department is rather anxious that she should not remain much longer in the Council's care. I understand that you are in regular employment and we'd like to think that you are making plans to have her with you."

"I can't have her yet," she replied, "I'm staying here with my sister and she won't let me bring the child here."

I looked about me; it seemed very unlikely that two such well-favoured women could be accommodated in so little space. She interpreted my glance and said: "We don't both live in this room; my sister has this downstairs flat and she lets me use this room."

"Wouldn't it be possible for you to find some other place where you could have the child with you?"

"Well, I work shifts, sometimes from seven to three in the day, or from three to ten at night. I couldn't look after her all the time."

"Miss Sweeney, many young women have the same problem. Some of them have solved it by taking jobs which leave them free during the evenings and weekends; the children are placed in a day nursery and can be with their mothers each evening."

"Yes, I know. I'll do that as soon as I can find a better job, working days only." Somehow I had the feeling that this was merely an excuse.

"Another thing, Miss Sweeney. It seems that so far you have not been making any contribution to Patricia's maintenance. She is being cared for at public expense, and either you or her father should take some responsibility in that direction."

"I'll pay something as soon as I can."

"And her father?"

"What about him?"

"If he is employed he should make a regular payment. I understand that he visits Patricia."

She sat quietly for a few moments.

"He's like you." I was somewhat unprepared for that; it was not clear whether she meant that he looked like me, or was of the same colour. On such short acquaintance I could think of no other basis for comparison.

"Oh, really?"

"He's from your part of the world. Barbados."

"I'm from British Guiana." I don't think the slight geographical variation was of much interest to her. Silence.

"Is he working?"

"Yes, he's on the Underground."

"Probably if I have a talk with him it might help," I said.

She stood up suddenly, crossed to the door, and opened it, as if half-expecting that someone may have been listening outside. Satisfied, she resumed her seat.

"Do you know where he lives?"

Again there was a pause as she considered the question. Then she said in a rush, "Yes. 34 Glencastle Street. It's off the Bayswater Road, near Notting Hill Gate Station."

If she knew where he lived and worked, why was it that the other Welfare Officer was unable to contact him? Miss Sweeney seemed willing to talk, so I asked: "How is it that you did not tell the other Officer where to find him?"

Silence again, then: "We weren't speaking to each other then."

I felt her reluctance to talk about it any more, so I changed the subject: "I haven't yet seen Patricia. How is she?"

Now she literally glowed. "She's fine. She's more like her daddy than me, 'cept perhaps her eyes. Would you believe it, she has eyes like mine. Grey." She said this with a sort of wonder, as if she'd never become fully accustomed to the fact. We laughed.

"I'll pay her a visit as soon as I can. If she has eyes like yours she's not doing too badly." We were getting along fine now, and when I was leaving we shook hands at the door, quite an improvement on my arrival. There was no sign of the sister.

I thought I'd press on to Notting Hill; perhaps I'd find him at home. Considering this, I suddenly realized that I did not know the young man's name; somehow in our discussion I'd completely forgotten to ask it. I hurried back and rang the bell. The sister answered the door, saying: "Well, what now?"

"I'm awfully sorry, but I've forgotten something."

She moved aside to let me pass and I hurried to Miss Sweeney's room.

"I'm afraid I forgot to ask the name of Patricia's father," I told her.

"Jason Griffiths. After you'd gone I wondered if I had told you, because I didn't tell the other one."

I couldn't understand why she needed to be so mysterious about the man, but hoped I'd get on well enough with him to find out.

Years ago I worked in East London; each day to reach my school I passed through a succession of dingy streets in depressing neighbourhoods, and wondered at the dignity and self-respect which grew and nourished there together with the other things, like wheat among the tares; it always seemed to me that each instance of honesty, graciousness and love must have been the result of a gigantic struggle against the general conspiracy of poverty and its attendant evils. I had the same feeling as I walked towards my destination from Notting Hill Gate Tube Station. This was what would probably be called a coloured community. The old terraced houses continued in nearly unbroken line along both sides of the street. The original paint had long ago disappeared under countless coatings of grime and soot, which summer's sun and winter's rain and snow had transformed into an ugly, greenish, scabrous skin, now curling away from the crumbling plaster in long, irregular flakes.

It was a lively street. People everywhere, nearly all of them black, and nearly all of them men. And cars. Some shiny new, being lovingly polished by their owners; others old, ramshackle, with their bonnets up, from which protruded denim-covered backsides and legs, as if the ancient vehicles had patiently waited for this moment and were now casually devouring those who had once mistreated them. Other men sat on the steps and casually joked with their neighbours, now and then erupting in a burst of laughter coming from deep within them, sweet to hear, a kind of bugling, richly defiant of the grime and poverty.

Someone once told me that these new citizens chose to live in these places. I think that is true, but, for reasons other than my informant preferred. On this balmy evening they could enjoy a short period of togetherness before retiring into their individual one-room castles; in the face of general discrimination and exclusion, there was some small measure of security among others similarly beset. But I knew that, for most of them, this was merely a staging post, a hold-over where one husbanded one's resources and planned the next move forward. Sometimes the hope and the planning were protracted to the point of inertia, but many of them still went through the motions out of sheer habit.

Several men sat on the steps of No. 34 and observed my approach, but with half-averted faces. I stopped, bade them "Good evening," and inquired for Mr Griffiths.

"Don't know if he's home," someone answered. "He lives below there, in the basement."

A short flight of stairs led downwards at right angles to the street. As I neared the bottom, a young man began mounting upward. He was dressed in the dark blue uniform of London Transport, neatly pressed and brushed and with shiny black shoes. He carried the uniform greatcoat folded over one arm and in the other a brown briefcase of plastic material.

"Excuse me," I addressed him, "but I'm looking for Mr Griffiths."

He looked up at me. "I'm Griffiths."

I had expected an older man, someone of perhaps thirty years or more. It seemed to me that this young man could be hardly more than twenty-two or three. Perhaps there was more than one Griffiths.

"I wonder if I may speak to you for a moment," I said, keeping my voice low; conversation from above stairs had slackened somewhat, and others might be interested in my business here.

"I'm just off to work," he replied. "What's it about?"

I stepped down until we were close together. "I'm from the Welfare Department. I'd like to talk to you about your little girl Patricia."

He was the right person, because his slim face brightened into a smile. "Oh, look, I've already locked up, but we can talk as we walk along if you like."

That was fine with me. At the top of the steps he exchanged a few words with the other men as we walked away, then, out of their hearing, he said: "How did you find me?"

"Miss Sweeney gave me your address."

"Brigid?" He exclaimed in surprise. "But she always said . . . " He did not finish the remark.

"I went to see her today. We had a long talk and I suggested that I should see you, so she told me where to find you."

E. R. BRAITHWAITE

"She's a funny one, that Brigid," he murmured, "a real case. She's Irish, you know. Sometimes I just can't figure her out. And that sister of hers. Did you meet her?"

"I saw her."

"A real case, that one. Look, I report for work at seven o'clock but I usually like to get there a bit early. Not far—Notting Hill Gate Station. We could go into the tea-shop next door for a coffee and talk there if you like."

I agreed. We hurried along the Bayswater Road, through the narrow footways between the huge L.C.C. building project which was transforming Notting Hill Gate, and into a Lyons tea-shop; even here the clang and grind of hydraulic hammers and drills and the unceasing rattle of concrete mixers filtered through and voices had to be pitched higher than normal to be heard.

"Funny thing," he began. "We met in this shop. She used to work here. I'd come in for a meal or coffee or something and I'd see her over there, behind the counter. She seemed very nice, you know, she'd smile or say 'Good afternoon' or something. Well, you know how it is, later on we got to chatting a bit, then one day I up and asked her if she'd go out with me." He smiled, remembering.

"She was always laughing, at everything. She told me she lived with an older sister, but she'd never let me go to her home. Never. I wasn't too keen for her to come to my place, you know, with the fellers always about and making cracks as soon as they see you with a woman, but there was nowhere else to go if we wanted to talk or things like that, and she said she didn't mind. Well, everything was fine until we knew the baby was coming. Then she started acting funny. I just don't know what came over her. She hardly wanted to talk to me. Then she told me she was going back to Ireland and wanted some money, so I asked her what about the baby. She said she'd come back when the baby was born. I argued with her but it was no use. That woman can be stubborn when she wants to. So I gave her money; I've saved a bit, you see. Well, my friend, I didn't hear another word from Brigid for months. It worried me, you know, wondering how she was getting on with the baby coming and all, so one day I went around to her sister's house." He laughed, shaking his head from side to side as the memories came flooding back.

"You should have seen that sister. She opened the door and stood there, like the Rock of Ages. I asked if Brigid lived there and she said, 'So you're the Mr Man. Well, she's back to Ireland', then slammed the door in my face. You know, I guess she was crazy angry because her sister was in the family way for a black man. Well, I thought, if that's the way they feel, to hell with them. So I never went back there. But it worried me though, I can tell you, especially as she used to tell me how hard the life was back there in Ireland."

"Well, the next thing I know, about a year after, one night I'm at home and there's a knock at the door. I open it and there is Brigid. Boy, women are funny! She just stands there and says 'Hello, Jason'. Well, I invite her in and then she tells me what happened. She went home to Dublin but came back to have the child. Her sister told her to put it in the Home and to have nothing more to do with me. So I told her what I thought of her sister and that if she didn't like the colour of my skin to hell with her. But man, it wasn't that. You know what all the trouble was about? Her age. She's thirty-five, although you wouldn't think so."

Like hell I wouldn't think so, I thought, remembering the strong, sturdy woman.

"Man, that woman went through all that, just because she's

older than me. She said her sister told her she ought to be ashamed of herself, that I was no more than a boy. She really felt ashamed. Man, you should've heard what I told her. After all, I was man enough to give her a child, so what was all the nonsense about being too young? That's why she didn't write to me when she was in hospital; she didn't want anyone to see that a boy had got her with child. Well, she told me where Patricia was, but only after I'd promised that I wouldn't tell any of the people there where I lived or anything. When I argued with her, you know what she said? She told me I was only the putative father, and had no real rights. Where the hell did she get that stuff? You know, sometimes I felt like belting her one. Anyway, what can you do? So I went to see the baby whenever I could."

Now his voice became very earnest.

"You know, Patricia is a lovely kid, and I'd like to take her out of the place. I've been after Brigid for nearly two years now to let me have the child. I've a married sister living in Kent who'd love to take care of her for me, but Brigid said no. That Brigid. She refuses to marry me or live with me and she won't let me have the child. Look, if she told you where to find me it means that she trusts you or something. Why don't you tell her that for the child's sake we ought to get married or something?"

I was surprised by the tenderness in his voice. This was no boy. This was a man willing and ready to shoulder his responsibilities.

"Could you support a wife and family?" I asked.

"Why not? I earn good money and I don't waste it. I could move away from where I'm living now and find some other place, and later on I could get a better job. I'm taking a correspondence course in electrical engineering," he tapped the briefcase with a finger, "I don't intend to work in the Underground all my life. Look at this."

From a pocket he took a thick, bulky wallet, from which he selected two Post Office Savings books. One of them bore his name, the other the name of Patricia Sweeney.

"Look at this," he repeated. "Since Pat was born I opened a savings account for her; instead of paying the money to the Government or the Council as you call them, I put it into her account each week. Look at it. Nobody made me do it, I did it myself. Why don't you talk to her?"

I promised that I would. I liked this young man; he seemed ambitious, decent and trustworthy. Perhaps my terms of reference did not include action such as he proposed, but if it would eventually lead to the child having a home with her parents then it was justified.

Next morning I wrote a letter to Brigid, inviting her to call at my office the following Saturday morning; I wrote a similar letter to Jason, although I did not indicate to either that the other would be present; if they found that out in advance of the day it would be because they had been in touch, and that was all to the good . . .

She arrived first, looking quite attractive in a two-piece suit of dark-green woolen material, set off by plain black calf shoes and a tight fitting little black hat which hid very little of her wavy blonde hair; now carefully made-up she looked more youthful than her thirty-odd years. I took her to one of the interview rooms and we chatted desultorily, me playing for time in the hope that he would come. She gave no hint of having seen him, so I guessed she did not know I expected him.

He was about ten minutes late. When I got the signal that I had a visitor, I left her to fetch him in. She was surprised to see him and blushed in some confusion; he took her presence easily in his stride, but there was no mistaking how delighted he was to see her. Without preamble I set things going.

"I have spoken with both of you separately and I thought that if we three got together we might be able to work something out for Patricia's benefit." I thought I'd play on their love for the child. "I don't suppose either of you have lived in an institution. From what I know of them I think they're not bad; they serve a useful and necessary function, for children who have no parents or whose parents are unable to provide a home for them. My job is to try to get children out of these Homes and either back with their own parents or with persons who are willing to assume the position and responsibilities of parents. Your daughter Patricia has spent an unnecessarily long time where she is. In the Council's opinion one or both of you could quite adequately take care of her. You're both employed and you both seem to have some affection for her. You, Miss Sweeney, could put her in a day nursery, and collect her each evening; on the other hand, Mr Griffiths assures me that his married sister is willing to take care of the child. So you see, either separately or together, you could provide her with a home."

"Well, what do you say, Brigid?" Jason asked. "Why can't we get married and have her with us?"

"Yes," she said. That's all, but I think her sudden and complete capitulation surprised him. He looked at her, open-mouthed, the arguments he had prepared subsiding in his mind, unnecessary now. All he could do was shake his head from side to side, too astonished for words. Finally: "What about your sister? She'll have a fit, you marrying a black man."

"You're wrong," Brigid countered, "She's nothing against your colour, 'twas just because you're younger than me."

Blushing furiously, she looked at me. At this distance from her sister she was not very formidable, in spite of her size.

"I'll leave you two to chat about it for a while," I said, "while I take a quick look at a few things upstairs. I'll be back in a few minutes."

About twenty minutes later I went back to them; they were both smoking and smiling at each other. They told me that they had discussed it all and were prepared to try and make a go of it.

They left my office together, arm in arm, smiling happily at each other, this oddly assorted couple, the slim youngster and the buxom Irish girl, and yet I had the feeling that it would all work out successfully. We could only wait and see.

Three weeks later Pat went home with them. I dropped in the following Sunday afternoon to see them. It was not an official call; I just happened to be in the vicinity and thought I'd call on them. Wonder of wonders! The elder sister was there, all dressed up, but very much at home in the small basement flat which shone with cleanliness and warmth. I had a cup of tea with them, Brigid's sister dominating the scene; evidently she had taken complete control of Pat, who spent her days with her instead of at the day nursery, until collected by Brigid each evening. People. Most of them had no idea of themselves and how much giving they were capable of; or perhaps they knew and were afraid to let themselves go.

There was just one point I had to clear up with Brigid; when I was able to chat alone with her for a moment I asked: "Why didn't you get the other Welfare Officer to see Jason? All this could have been settled long ago."

"It's the way they look at you as soon as they know you have a child by a black man," she replied. "I just didn't want them talking to Jason, they'd think he's ever so young, and besides, he's got a very nasty temper when he's roused. When you came I thought you'd understand."

My next case seemed quite hopeless. The file read:

Institution:	Falconbridge Residential Home
Children:	Diane Cosson. Age: Thirteen years
	Evelyn Cosson. Age: Twelve years
	Marian Cosson. Age: Nine years
	Victor Cosson. Age: Seven years
Mother:	Helen Grace Cosson (Mrs). Whereabouts unknown.
Father:	George Cosson. West Indian. Once operated a barber shop in Brixton; now serving a three-year prison sentence in Manchester
Welfare Officer:	Miss O. Spendler

From various comments in the file it appeared that Mrs Cosson had deserted the children about eighteen months previously; the father had applied to the Council to have them taken into care temporarily while he completed arrangements for them to be sent to his parents in British Guiana, but seven months after they were in residence at Falconbridge, he was imprisoned on a charge of living on the immoral earnings of a prostitute. No further action had so far been taken about the children's future.

They were told that their father was ill and would be unable to see them for some time: the two younger children had soon become adjusted to the new life, but the elder girls repeatedly inquired about his continued absence and the oldest one often was heard weeping in bed at night. The Welfare Officer who dealt with the case had twice written to Mr Cosson, but received no answer from him.

I went to see Miss Spendler, a short, bustling, jovial person, round-faced, with a quick, infectious smile and restless brown eyes; her handshake was very firm and powerful.

"I'm worried about those kids, Mr Braithwaite," she came directly to the point, "especially the eldest girl. Apparently she worshipped her father and now that he is so long absent, she's taking it hard. I wrote twice to him at the prison, suggesting that he write to them, either directly or through me, but he's never replied. Probably ashamed or something."

"What about their mother? Don't they inquire about her also?"

"I wondered about that, too, and asked their housemother. They're all together in the same cottage with a few other children in the care of a housemother. She says all their talk is about their father and what he used to do for them; take them to the park and the cinema, or buy them this and that. Hardly a mention of their mother, even when they first went to Falconbridge."

"Anything known about her?"

"Not much. The father didn't come to us until nearly a month after she left. Seems that he tried to manage the home himself, but it was too much for him. When I took on the case I spoke with some of the neighbours. They said she kept the children clean and fed, but spent a lot of time away from the house. Then one day she was seen leaving with a suitcase while her husband was at work and the children in school. Nobody had seen her since. The neighbours all seemed to be very much in sympathy with Mr Cosson."

"Was Mrs Cosson West Indian?"

"No. English. The children are really lovely kids."

"So his detention has nothing to do with his wife?"

"Oh, no. Apparently that happened after she left. He seemed quite a respectable person when he came here to see us about the children, but you can never tell with people. I can't understand why they do it, the women, I mean. If they must degrade themselves by becoming prostitutes, why do they then give the money to some man?"

"Did you attend the hearing?"

"Me? No. We knew nothing about it until after he was sentenced. I suppose he said nothing to them about his children until he knew he was going to prison. One of the staff here, Mr Cobley, who deals with probation cases, made some inquiries. Apparently the police were on to Mr Cosson for some time. Several women were giving him money, and some of them carried on their business in a room where he lived over his barber shop."

While she spoke, the name 'Cosson' rang tantalizing bells, barely audible, on the edge of memory. Cosson, Cosson. Then I got it. Of course, it was the same fellow. I'd met him briefly about two years earlier. Briefly, but not pleasantly. One day I had tried, unsuccessfully to get a haircut; at two barber's shops I had been told, quite courteously, by the barbers, that they had had no experience with Negro heads and were unwilling to take a chance. An acquaintance had given me the address of a barber's shop in Brixton, where, he assured me, I would have just the haircut I needed. Hopefully I found my way there, undeterred by the sordid locality and the grimy exterior of the shop. I opened the door and walked in. It was awful. The interior complemented the outside with its chronic untidiness and claustrophobic, depressing discomfort, its stale cigarette smoke and body odours.

Several black men were in the shop, sitting on rickety chairs against the walls, arguing loudly and heatedly about Britain and the discriminatory behaviour of the Jumbles (a corruption of John Bulls). Of the two barber's chairs, one was empty, the other was occupied by a black client on whose head the barber was busy with comb and clicking scissors. The instruments in his hands were all that distinguished him from the others in the room; he was of medium height, a light-skinned Negro badly in need of a shave himself, with the dead butt of a cigarette resting lightly on the corner of his lower lip, and bobbing up and down as he contributed his observations to the general argument. He wore unpressed grey slacks and a check cotton shirt, the front of which was powdered from the droppings of his cigarette ash, and my eyes followed the rolled-up shirt sleeves, along the light brown arms to the slim agile fingers, noting the blackened fingernails, and the dirty napkin tied around the client's neck. The floor was littered with discarded cigarette ends, hair and a thick accumulation of dust. I stood within the doorway taking it all in, then the barber looked around at me and nodded towards a vacant chair.

"Sit down, pal."

Obediently I seated myself. Gradually my attention swung from the room and its other occupants to myself, and anger began a slow boil inside me. What the hell was I doing in this place? 'Sit down, pal,' he had said, with the casual assurance that I would sit down, that I would accept the crummy place and his own untidy person, and wait patiently for his attention. Why? Why? I asked myself, only half-hearing the rise and fall of the voices around me. Was I accepting this filthy place so obediently, merely because it was operated by a Negro? Did I need a haircut so badly that I was prepared to forgo every hygienic standard? Would I have been prepared to accept the same from a white barber? My anger mounted as the full meaning of my surroundings struck me. This barber probably did not give a damn about me or any of the rest of us who were waiting for his attention. He was doing us no favour. The prices marked up on a fly-specked notice on the wall were the same as those in barber's shops where the attendants were smart in clean, white smocks, the instruments constantly sterilized, the floor regularly swept and the general hygienic standard high. He knew that English barbers were often either unfamiliar with Negro heads or disinclined to accommodate them; he guessed correctly that many black men, in Brixton and farther afield, had little alternative to his services, so he virtually had a captive clientele. Yes, maybe this fellow knew that most of us would be forced to come to him, so he saw no reason to put himself out for our accommodation.

Or perhaps, another thought intruded, the bastard knew no better. He may have learned his trade in similar crude surroundings, had never known anything better, and was merely continuing in a familiar pattern. It was easy for me to backtrack through the years to memories of British Guiana. There were barber's shops of all types, some elegant, others mediocre, and others little more than a crudely assembled tin shack with a smooth dirt floor. But memory was strong on one point. They were kept clean. The nicest were the open-air ones, just a chair or packing-case under a spreading mango tree and the barber was in business on Sunday mornings. Perhaps this man was attempting to transpose that sort of casual, catch-as-catch-can situation to the English scene . . .

Snatches of the conversation got through to me, the all too familiar chorus of complaints . . . "the Jumbles don't like us, Man,"

"They won't rent me a room, Man," on and on and on, while they sat in this sty without seeing the filth. Christ, if this barber *liked* them and treated them in this way, what should they not expect from people who disliked them, or hated them. I was now really angry, mostly with myself for letting him do this to me. I stood up. I had had enough.

"What's up, pal?" the barber asked.

"I'm leaving," I replied, coldly and pointedly.

"What's your hurry? I'm nearly finished here and you're next. These Spades are only shooting the breeze." He nodded towards the talkative men, all of whom laughed heartily at his reference to them as 'Spades'. Funny, they'd laugh when he called them spades, but the sparks would fly if a white man made a similar remark.

"I've changed my mind," I answered. I suppose my manner and tone of voice reflected my displeasure, but I did not care. Conversation around me slowed down and then died, as they all turned to stare at me. Down inside I knew that I should walk out without further comment, but some perverse inclination kept me there, insisting that I make my protest somehow.

"So what did you come here for?" the barber asked, his voice still slow and casual, his eyes assessing me with calculated indifference.

"A haircut."

"Then sit down, if that's what you want."

"I don't think I'll bother," I replied, deliberately looking around the shop, that he might not mistake my meaning.

"Then f—k you, pal." He returned his attention to his work. I opened the door and walked out, closing it on the thick hostility which had so suddenly been generated in the room. I don't suppose my gesture meant a damned thing to him, yet I felt better for having made it. Probably the others hated me for it; they might so easily have considered it as snobbishness on my part, as another instance of 'uppitiness' by those black men who, with a little education, looked down their noses at their humbler brethren. Oh, well, to hell with them and what they thought. If they imagined that the situation of which they complained would improve itself magically while they sat on their arses and grumbled they'd have a long wait. If they did not mind the dirt and stink in the barber's shop, probably they might not mind it in their homes. When they acquired guts enough to demand higher standards among themselves, and the self-respect to insist on those standards, they would take the first steps towards earning the respect of the host community.

With these thoughts rampant in my mind, I caught a train to Victoria, then travelled by Underground to Bond Street to make a few purchases at one of the large department stores in Oxford Street; while shopping I noticed a sign 'Gentlemen's Hair-dressers, Third Floor.' I went up, was courteously received and served, and it cost no more than I would have paid at Brixton.

Now, listening to Miss Spendler, I remembered the shop, the man and the name. It was Cosson. Small world.

"What is it that the Council wants to do in this case? From reading the file I could see that things had reached an impasse, but I wasn't sure what was expected of me."

"Before Mr Cosson went to prison he had been trying to get his children sent to their grandparents. Perhaps, everything considered, it would be the best thing for them. Maybe you could get in touch with him and see whether it can be arranged?"

"Were the children all born in Britain?"

"Yes."

"If, as you say, they are so attached to their father, it might not be an easy thing to sort of pack them off to strangers whom they have never seen, no matter what the relationship."

"But it might be better for them to be among their own people," she said. I did not feel in the mood to discuss that.

"I think I'll see the children, then arrange to visit the father in prison. I'll let you know what happens."

"Best of luck, Mr Braithwaite."

Falconbridge lay deep in the Sussex countryside, a collection of pleasant, red-brick houses dispersed over several acres of meadow-land. Tall, spreading oak-trees, rough lawns and flowering shrubs and the warm afternoon sunlight conspired to present an air of peace and contentment; somehow I had expected something different, less orderly. A network of paved roadways led from the main adminis-tration building through shady trees to the houses, each of which was centrally divided to accommodate two 'families', a housemother and her children; each residence had a nameboard on the door. The Cossons lived in 'Perivale House'. The housemother, Miss Bancroft, answered my knock and invited me into a comfortable room which bore all the signs of being used by many children; it was disorderly, but pleasant and relaxing. I explained the reason for my visit.

The children were all at school, but were expected in soon after four o'clock; the youngest ones came in first—they were at the local junior school. The others attended school in the town, so they trav-elled by bus. She invited me to stay to tea, when I would be able to talk to them.

She was a cheery, ample person, with a broad face and short, pale hair. She chatted on about the children in her care, what they did, how they were progressing at school, the easy ones, the difficult ones; but she spoke as if they were all her children, her own flesh and blood.

"I've just taken over the Cossons, and I'm hoping to see their father soon, to discover if he still plans to send them to British Guiana," I said.

Immediately some of the warmth seemed to evaporate from our easily established rapport. "I heard that Mr Cosson had thought about it," she replied, "but I took it for granted, after all this time, that he had given up the idea. After all, these children were born here in England, they grew up here, and I don't think they would like it in Africa. I mean, it won't be fair to them."

"British Guiana is in South America, not Africa," I said.

"It's still foreign, isn't it?" she replied. "They're comfortable here, they live in a house, go to school, and I take care of them. It would be cruel to send them to a foreign country, where you don't know how they'll live or what they'll eat or anything. They've been talking to me about it and I know they didn't like the idea of being sent away to any foreign place."

It was clear that she didn't like the idea at all; and I suspected that whatever talking had been done on the matter was initiated by herself.

"I'm merely looking into it. Whatever is decided about the children's future must be their father's responsibility."

"If what the papers said about him is true, then they're better off here, without him. They're lovely kids, and it's a shame their father has to behave like that."

"How are they getting on at school? The older ones?" I thought if safer to keep away from discussion of the children's future until I knew more about Mr Cosson's plans.

Once again this set her off in lively praise of the girls; both were at the local Grammar school, and to hear Miss Bancroft tell it, they were the double-distilled quintessence of intelligence and good conduct.

"And the others?"

"That Victor is a card." The way in which she said it clearly indicated that the boy occupied a very special place in her heart. "He's not as clever as the others and he can be so stubborn when he chooses! But he's a lovable child."

We chatted about the other children in her charge and got along fine until the children arrived. I was introduced to them as a friend of their father, which I thought was going it a bit steep, especially as this caused the Cosson children to ask me a million questions about their father, most of which I tried to parry, with evasive replies. Desperately I exploited my forthcoming visit to him, and suggested that they each write a letter which I promised to deliver.

Miss Bancroft had not exaggerated in her remarks about the children; they were sturdy, bright and well-mannered; Victor, the youngest, was inclined to show off in order to attract attention to himself; but this is a normal characteristic for the smallest member of any family group. Diane, the eldest, was a lovely, shy child; like the other two girls, she wore her wavy brown hair in two thick plaits which hung halfway down her back. Her skin was pale *café au lait,* and her large brown eyes shone behind long, curling lashes.

"Is my Daddy still too ill to write?" she asked me.

"He has been, but he is recovering and I'm sure you'll get a letter soon from him."

It sickened me, having to lie to these children, and I made a mental note to say a few things to their father when I met him; he could, at least, write to them through Miss Bancroft, and thus avoid whatever embarrassment he feared from a prison postmark.

When tea was ready we all sat down, ten of us; the Cossons, four other children, Miss Bancroft and myself. The conversation was lively and very entertaining. The housemother asked them about the day's events in school and encouraged them to express themselves. The more I listened to the group, the more I began to appreciate the truth of an observation someone had made at the Kinsmans'. "Put an adult and some children together in a congenial atmosphere and you're well on the way to creating a family." This was a family; furthermore, any attempt to disrupt it would not be happily received. Miss Bancroft was a paid servant, but the Council was receiving something from her which it could not buy, and, watching her, it occurred to me that she too was receiving something—perhaps the affection and love which the children might otherwise have given to their parents.

When tea was over the children collected the dishes and formed wash-up and drying teams while I had a further chat with Miss Bancroft.

"What do you think of them?" she asked.

"I'd like to congratulate you, Miss Bancroft; you're doing a wonderful job with them."

"It's easy." She was evidently pleased with my remark.

"I'm sure Mr Cosson will be very pleased to know they are getting on so well."

"I don't suppose he cares, or he would surely have written to them or something."

Outside the very air had changed; now it was jocund with the laughter and shrill cries of children at play; safe, happy children. On my way to the main gate I saw them in groups, boys and girls, skipping, playing football, rolling about on the grass or juggling rubber balls expertly against a wall.

Next morning I wrote a letter to the Welfare Officer at Strangeways Prison, Manchester, explaining the situation and asking permission to visit Mr Cosson; at the same time I wrote to Mr Cosson, introducing myself as the Welfare Officer dealing with the case, and indicating that I would soon be calling to see him. In this way, I thought, he'll either see me, or he'd have to give the prison Welfare Officer a damn good reason for declining . . . .

Chapter
Seven

Bᴠ ᴀʀʀᴀɴɢᴇᴍᴇɴᴛ ᴛʜᴇ ᴛᴀᴍᴇʀʟᴀɴᴇs picked me up at my office soon after two o'clock on Saturday afternoon, and we drove out to Franmere. I sat in front beside Mr Tamerlane; behind me the two girls were like jumping beans in their excitement, asking all kinds of questions about Roddy, to which I could not possibly give answers. It seemed as though they wanted quickly to bridge the gap between not knowing and knowing him, to draw him into the family circle with the least possible delay. I rather suspect that their parents were equally excited, especially Mr Tamerlane. He was just too concerned with other things—the sparkplugs needed cleaning, time to change the oil in the crank-case—anything except what lay at the end of the trip.

Matron was waiting for us and ushered us into her office. She chatted with them about the Home and the children, and the usual pattern of visiting.

"We like the parents to come here and be with the child for an hour or two at first; then, as they get to know and accept each other, the child can be taken out for an afternoon, then later for a weekend visit, to see how he'll settle in at what is likely to be his new home. We like this to be quite unhurried, so that it could be discontinued without too much bother if there's any indication that it might fail."

Mr and Mrs Tamerlane were listening quite patiently to this; I could hardly refrain from laughter as I watched the girls trying bravely to restrain their impatience, sitting there, well-mannered and outwardly quiet. I knew that Matron was carefully watching them all, getting the 'feel' of them, so to speak. She chatted a little with the girls, about school, then said: "Roddy's outside with the rabbits; I'll take you to him."

I followed them as far as the doorway to the backyard, then watched as the group converged on Roddy who was squatted on the rough lawn feeding two tame rabbits with lettuce leaves; momentarily he looked pathetically small beside them, in spite of the wide-legged stance which he assumed on rising to meet them. I walked away in the opposite direction, through an alley and down a narrow walled lane. Later I returned to see him squatted in the same place with the girls, all three in serious discussion about something closely related to their private world.

Indoors I found John and Ella in Matron's office; Ella looked quite pleased and excited, "He's marvellous," she said.

To put some slight curb on their enthusiasm I mentioned that there were a few difficulties likely to be encountered with the Middlesex Council, but assured them that the Supervisor was working on that end.

"One thing I should mention," Matron said. "Recently Roddy got himself a foster-aunt, as you might say. A Miss Keriham. Would you have any objections to her visiting him occasionally? They seem to get on quite well and I feel sure she'd like to keep in touch with him even after he leaves here."

They both said they had no objections, and Ella added: "What's she like, Miss Keriham?"

"Very nice," Matron replied. "Ask Mr Braithwaite, he brought her."

Without replying I excused myself and went out to the children, who greeted me with loud excited cries, each wanting to tell me something. Before long I noticed that Roddy too was calling me 'Uncle Ricky', quickly following the pattern set by June and Jacqueline. Looking at the three of them I wished desperately that nothing would occur to spoil this chance, but everything was working so smoothly that it worried me somewhat.

Before leaving, we told Roddy that the Tamerlanes would take him to their home for tea the following Saturday; that was to give him something pleasurable to think about and also to assure him that he'd see his new friends again, soon.

I telephoned Olga that evening to inform her of these developments; at least that, I argued to myself, was my reason for telephoning. I told her about the Tamerlanes and anticipated her queries by assuring her that there would be no objections to her continued visits to Roddy even when he left Franmere.

On Monday I received a reply from the Welfare Officer at Strangeways Prison. I would be welcome to visit Mr Cosson; enclosed was a short note from Mr Cosson thanking me for my letter and expressing his wish to see me. I travelled to Manchester the next morning. In the same compartment were three men, two of whom were, from their conversation, representatives of an important firm of industrial engineers, on their way to a conference; the other person's face was quite familiar, and after a little while I remembered seeing it regularly on television; he was one of a panel of experts who, each Sunday, discussed questions of topical interest. The rest of the week he was a Member of Parliament for a constituency not very far from London. Both he and I tried to read our newspapers, and I suspected that we experienced the same difficulties of concentration because of the uninhibited way in which our dynamic fellow-travellers reviewed recent occasions on which they had managed to impose their views on resistant but less imaginative colleagues. Between bouts of reading and gazing through the window at the same grey, dull, flitting scene, I slept fitfully, and had not realized that the two engineers had left, until I felt the protracted silence.

Opening my eyes I met those of the M.P., who smiled and said: "Rather quiet, don't you think?"

I got his meaning and we both laughed. From there on we fell into conversation. I told him I recognized his face and we talked about television and its effect on public information, entertainment and taste. He made his observations with the same suave, slightly detached professorial air which I had remarked so often, and which was rather pleasing at closer quarters.

As the train crawled into the deeper gloom of Manchester Station we collected our macs and papers, preparing to leave, and he said: "This has been a most delightful chat, Braithwaite most delightful. Oddly enough, it is the first time I've sat and chatted with a Negro. I hope we meet again sometime."

Somehow, that spoiled it for me, and all the way to the prison his words kept repeating themselves in my mind. This suave, intelligent, informed man, an elected representative of the people, making a remark like that in the year of Our Lord 1958. I was not sure if it was intended as a boast or confession. I thought of the location of his constituency; I knew that many coloured families lived there. They were part of it; they very probably worked in it, their children were at school in it, some of them surely voted in it. Yet he had never talked with one of them. Probably because none of them had ever sought him out personally for help or advice on a personal matter. But was that the only basis for a relationship between the Member of Parliament and those who elected him? Should he always wait until some personal crisis forced them to seek him out? Was it not also his business and his responsibility deliberately to seek to know as many of his constituents as possible? Did he even know that there were coloured people among his constituents?

Perhaps I was letting my imagination run riot, discolouring an ordinary pedestrian remark. But the idea persisted that, in spite of the deep social malaise which occasionally erupted in inter-racial violence and disorder, this man, and probably others, had not considered it worth his while to meet some of the people concerned, in an attempt to understand the root causes, because in the normal processes of his professional duties he would certainly find himself discussing the symptoms.

Maybe, I further argued to myself, he considered his constituency sufficiently distant from the centres of reported troubles, to remain free and isolated from those ugly, dramatic circumstances. Perhaps if I had known earlier that our conversation represented something new in his experience, I might have put a flea in his ear, so to speak. Then I thought, that, after all, our conversation represented nothing more or less than a discourse between two men, conducted in terms of equality and respect; for whatever reason he made his parting remark, I should not attach too much importance to it. When we parted he had been smiling broadly, apparently really pleased about our encounter; yet I found myself thinking of the old days when elderly people in the East End of London reached forward to shake hands with me, just for the luck which they believed would result. Well, good luck to him too.

At the prison I was shown to the Welfare Officer's office; we chatted awhile, then he sent an orderly to fetch Mr Cosson. In the meantime the Welfare Officer spoke of Mr Cosson as a model prisoner during the eighteen months he had so far spent at Strangeways; if he continued in the same way he was likely to be released in a little over two years; he worked in the prison barber's shop, in order to maintain his proficiency against the time of his release. As I listened to him I hoped that the standards in the prison barber's shop were such that Mr Cosson would learn a few lessons on cleanliness.

He had changed little. The drab prison uniform was worn with the same casual arrogance, though it hung loosely about his spare frame; but it was the same barber of the brief Brixton interlude. If he recognized me, he gave no sign. I introduced myself and we shook hands. The Welfare Officer said we could have our chat in his office; if Mr Cosson preferred it, he could leave us to speak privately. Mr Cosson quickly indicated that he would prefer the Welfare Officer to remain, reminding him that he already knew everything about his affairs, so there was nothing secret to be said. Hearing this I said my piece, stating first that the Council was concerned to know whether he intended to pursue his earlier plan to send the children to his parents in British Guiana; then I said that with no sign of the mother, and himself out of circulation for some time, the children were rather insecure, especially as he had, so far, refused to communicate with them.

Watching him, as I spoke, I got the impression that he was watching the prison Welfare Officer, as if gauging his reaction to my remarks. When he finally spoke he completely surprised me. I suppose it is natural to expect that any period of imprisonment produces some change in a man or woman, but I was unprepared for the whining tone in which he attempted to defend himself. He blamed his wife for all his misfortunes, expressed his love for his children, claimed that he did not write to them primarily for their own sake, because he did not want any taint of prison life to reach them, even through a letter. But he insisted that he missed them terribly, dreamed frequently of them, and missed them even more after each dream. He said that his immediate ambition was to see them; his good conduct record in prison would probably justify a short two-day parole to allow him to visit them, providing someone on the 'outside' would be willing to guarantee him accommodation for that period.

Perhaps I do him grave injustice, but I had the feeling that his obsequious humility was completely phoney, put on for the benefit of the prison official and myself, in order to achieve the two-day parole. The 'somebody on the outside' was evidently myself, and his professed concern and love for his children was the lever. He had me nicely in a corner.

"Is it true about the parole?" I asked the Welfare Officer.

"Yes. Providing a prisoner's conduct is satisfactory over a reasonable period of time, he may apply for such a parole on compassionate grounds. But some responsible person must give a written guarantee of board and lodging, and an assurance that the prisoner will return at the end of the parole."

It occurred to me that Mr Cosson knew all this, had been fully briefed about it, probably by prisoners who knew all the ropes. I said that, as a Council employee, I could not undertake to offer any guarantees without the Council's express authority. Although it would be a pleasant thing to have Mr Cosson visit his children, my business was to discover whether he still intended to send his children to British Guiana, or, if not, what alternative plans had he got for them?

"I think I've changed my mind about sending them home," he replied. "They'd be better off here in England where I could keep an eye on them, and they'd have the chance of a good education. When I get out I could find a job or maybe start another shop and after a while have them with me."

This was said in the same persistent, whining voice which somehow I found very off-putting. I felt prompted to ask: "Would you be able to raise the funds necessary to open another shop?"

"Yes," he replied, quickly. "I've got some friends who'd stake me, you know; all I'd need is enough to open a shop and buy some furniture and equipment."

"Perhaps one of them could be your guarantor for the parole."

"Well, not exactly," the Welfare Officer intervened. "Guarantors are only accepted from certain specific categories of persons."

I got the message. I was in a category marked "Acceptable". Then an idea occurred to me. "Perhaps Mr Cosson can get in touch with the Migrants' Division of the West Indies Commission," I suggested. "They might be able to help and advise on the question of repatriating the children and might even make some suggestions about guaranteeing his parole."

I must have touched on something, an exposed nerve in the carefully arranged persona, for a flash of the Cosson I had first met showed itself. "They're no damned good, those people. Oh, excuse me, Sir," this was more to the prison officer than to me. "I've written to them time and again, but they say they can't do anything for me. They wanted to write and tell my parents I'm in jail, and ask them if they'd have the children, but I refused to let them do it. Those black big-shots know how to talk, that's all."

"Well, as I've already told you, Mr Cosson, I cannot promise you anything. I'll put the matter to the authorities when I return to London and, if they think it is in the best interests of the children for you to visit them, they may decide to take some action. I can promise you no more than that, except that I will write to you promptly after discussing the matter in London."

Soon afterwards Mr Cosson left us.

"Do you think your people will agree to standing as guarantor for him?" the prison official asked.

"It seems unlikely, but I'll inquire. I don't know if there is any precedent for it."

"From what you say, the children, especially the eldest girl, miss him. Won't it be a good thing for him to see her, and the others?"

"It most certainly would, but I don't know whether the Council would consider that a good enough reason for guaranteeing a prisoner's parole."

More than that I would not say, and left soon afterwards, still somewhat doubtful about Mr Cosson's sincerity.

Next day I discussed the matter with the Supervisor, taking care to let no hint of my own reservations prejudice Mr Cosson's position. She took a completely different view.

"This matter of a guarantee is utter nonsense. If we agree to it and, while he is out he commits some misdemeanour, they could not possibly blame us for it. They must assume that it is reasonably assured that Mr Cosson will spend the two days away and return to prison without jeopardizing his chances of an early release, so I think we too can take a chance on him, providing we can be sure he will visit the children. Do you know of any person who would accommodate him for the time?"

I didn't know of anyone, but I promised to inquire around.

"Who'll pay for it?" I asked her.

"I suppose we will," she said. "We could justify it on the grounds of its advantage to the children. Another thing, I have news on the Rodwell Williams case. Middlesex are digging their heels in, both on the money and our poaching on their preserves, so I'm taking the matter higher up. I've had a talk with our people at County Hall and they're prepared to back us up all the way. Have the Tamerlanes met him yet?"

"Yes, they were all there last Saturday."

"Good. I see no reason why they should not go ahead getting to know each other. Well, see what you can do about Mr Cosson."

Before my office colleagues disappeared on their various rounds I mentioned to them that I wanted to find temporary accommodation—two days, for a prisoner on ticket-of-leave, in the hope that one of them might know someone who knew someone who could rent me a room.

After some discussion back and forth, Miss Drake remarked: "If you have any difficulty getting him a room I know somewhere you might try," and she scribbled an address on a slip of paper. "They're not coloured, but I don't suppose they'd mind renting him a room, especially if we recommend him."

This was generally characteristic of the Welfare Officers whom I met, either as close colleagues or at occasional consultations; this readiness to help, to share a colleague's problem. At times I disagreed with them about certain concepts or attitudes, especially where coloured people were concerned, but whenever I needed their help or advice, it was immediately available, without exception.

The slip of paper Miss Drake had given me carried no telephone number, so I decided to drop around and see the couple, Mr and Mrs Redmond, at 63 Windsor Drive, Pimlico.

It was an unpretentious terrace house, in a quiet side street. Now and again I come upon these places, sudden oases in the heart of one of the world's largest cities; quiet, as if long ago there had been a successful conspiracy among all kinds of vehicular traffic to boycott the place. The inhabitants themselves seemed to be conditioned to the situation and I noticed that a milk roundsman placed some bottles very carefully down beside a door as if reluctant to disturb the prevailing peace by a solitary clink.

Mrs Redmond opened the door to my knock, and seemed a bit startled to discover a black caller on her doorstep. As so often happens, she asked me a question: "Yes?" she said. One of these days someone will think up a fitting reply to that one. To me it generally indicates a mixture of surprise, fear, and distrust.

"I'm from the Welfare Department," I said. "Miss Drake, one of the Welfare Officers, suggested that I come to see you."

"Oh, Miss Drake. Oh, yes. Won't you come in?" Mention of Miss Drake's name had reassured her, now she smiled, and I realized that any housewife would have reacted in very much the same way if confronted by a stranger on her doorstep.

She led me to a large warm room where her husband was busy with several cages of yellow canaries, some of which were twittering excitedly as they hopped about their perches. I introduced myself and quickly told them my business. I merely stated that Mr

Cosson was in prison, but said nothing about the crimes which had taken him there. I explained that the Department was guaranteeing his short parole because of his children, and that we would pay the charges for the room.

"Would he require meals?" Mrs Redmond asked. I had not thought about that, but I might as well go the whole way.

"It would help, if it would not be inconvenient for you," I said.

"No inconvenience at all," she assured me.

So far they had not asked me the one question I had been expecting to hear, so I raised it.

"Mr Cosson is black."

"We more or less gathered that," Mr Redmond said, as casually as he might have remarked on the weather. Then his wife mentioned an inclusive figure for Mr Cosson's board and lodging for the two nights, surprisingly low. I accepted and left, after promising to let them know when he was expected to arrive.

Later that day I wrote to the Welfare Officer at the prison, informing him that I was empowered to act as guarantor for Mr Cosson, and giving details of the accommodation arranged. I wrote, at the same time, to Mr Cosson, saying very much the same thing. After hearing from him I would let the Matron at Falconbridge know about his intended visit so that she could prepare the children to meet him . . .

Just as I was packing up for the day the telephone operator rang through to say a lady had called to see me and was in the waiting-room. Not my best time of day, and I went downstairs hoping to get it over with as quickly as possible. To my surprise, it was Miss Bruce. Motherhood certainly seems to bring out the best of some women, investing them with a certain special beauty and seren-ity. Her full figure was smartly set off by a simple dress of grey wool, her wavy hair was attractively arranged in a high chignon (I guessed there was Indian admixture somewhere along the line). The face was smooth, girlish, bright eyed, with the barest trace of lipstick on the wide, full mouth. Looking at her now, no one would imagine that she was the mother of three children, and was faced with more than a bucketful of problems.

"Hello, Mr Braithwaite."

"It's good to see you looking so well, Miss Bruce. How are things with you?"

"Not too bad." Low voiced. And rather defenceless. A veritable sitting duck. The kind of woman who has to have a man to lean on, and will try and try again.

"How's the baby?"

"He's fine, but he's in a nursery. The hospital people fixed it up for me. You see, the landlord wouldn't let me have the room again; the hospital people went to see him, but he said I couldn't bring the baby back with me. The Almoner told me to ask you if you could arrange for Charles—that's the baby's name, Charles Albert—for him to go to the same place as Ann and Yvonne, so I can visit them together. As soon as I am better I will get a job and try to find a room where I can have them all with me."

God, how naïve she was. Find a job and a room big enough for the four of them. One weak woman and three helpless infants. She'd never do it, by herself. She wasn't the type, at least she didn't seem to be. But, sometimes these weak-looking people could exhibit amazing reserves of fortitude. One never knew.

"I'll see what I can do about it, Miss Bruce."

"I would like to visit the twins, but . . . " She paused in embarrassment, and I felt sure she was blushing, invisibly. I guessed the reason.

"We could arrange for you to travel down there," I said. "I'll go upstairs and get you some money for your return bus and train fare to the nursery at Brighton."

This was one of our services, to provide funds in cases such as this, that the contact between parent and child be maintained.

"Give the girls a kiss for me," I said when she was leaving.

Next morning I went to the Migrants' Services Division, a subsection of the Colonial Office directly concerned with West Indian immigrants, and staffed mainly by West Indians. I wanted to discover the circumstances which would surround Mr Cosson's efforts to send his children to British Guiana, providing he still intended pursuing that course.

I was most courteously received at the Division, and spent a little time in pleasant chit-chat with several of the staff, many of whom are my personal friends. I did not mention Mr Cosson by name, but presented a hypothetical case closely parallel to his, and inquired whether the Migrants' Division, could, if asked, take any action in the matter. Before replying they sat me down and gathered around, to give me what they called 'a briefing' on the way the Migrants' Division operated, taking impromptu turns, like members of a closely integrated dance-band.

First and foremost I was to get it straight that the Migrants' Division was not a Welfare organization for West Indians, although that misunderstanding was widespread both in Britain and the West Indies and they rather suspected that I entertained a similar idea of its purpose. The only services it provided and was intended to provide were advisory and liaison-advisory in helping migrants, especially new arrivals, to adjust to the unfamiliar conditions of housing, employment, food and clothing, and liaison in putting them in touch, when necessary, with the National Agency or departments which could be of most help to them.

Most of the staff had lived in Britain for many years; some were educated here or had served with the Armed Forces; they were all very knowledgeable about the problems likely to be encountered by immigrants, and spent an appreciable amount of their time travelling about the country meeting groups of West Indians wherever they were to be found, discussing with them their problems, helping them to settle down. They seized every opportunity offered to talk with English people about the new arrivals, and some not so new, in attempts to bridge the social, cultural and educational gaps which often presented themselves, sometimes in rather hazardous and unhappy circumstances.

None of this was really new to me, but I let them tell me; presently I had a few questions which could well be brought into this friendly discussion without any risk of suspicion of censure. Here they were, bright, educated men and women, ideally representative of the various racial origins and admixture of those origins, which make up the populations of the Caribbean areas; from Jamaica, Trinidad, British Guiana, and other islands. They worked together in an easy harmony which had as its basis a similarity of interest in purposeful, helpful service. I knew that they took themselves and their work very seriously, but I also knew that, among West Indians in general, and those hardest hit by the twin scourge of prejudice and discrimination in particular, this image of the Migrants' Division and its officials was either badly blurred or distorted. I slipped my piece into a temporary break in the conversation.

"Sometimes West Indians come to my office with problems which are somewhat outside the general scope of my work, problems which, it seems to me, could be better dealt with by this division, but they invariably resist any suggestion that they come to see you. As a matter of fact, I hear many reports critical of the attitude and conduct of the Migrants' Division."

The most senior official present replied to this. He too had heard unfavourable comment about the Division, but blamed it on the lack of proper information about its operation, on the one hand, and the fact that, for those West Indians who found themselves in difficulty, kind words and a sympathetic ear were not nearly enough, and the absence of more practical help all to easily favoured bitterness and dissatisfaction.

"We are Civil Servants," he said, "and as such are subject to all the bureaucratic limitations which that term implies, but because we are West Indians, our needy compatriots expect much more of us than we are able to give."

Finally they got around to discussing my hypothetical problem case, examining, for my benefit, the several difficulties contained. First of all, it was not a matter of repatriation, because all the children were born in England, of an English mother, and providing she had not lost or changed her citizenship, they were legally English. Also, before they could be moved, their mother's permission in writing was necessary, or, failing that, it must be fully established that she had completely deserted the children to their father's care, thus leaving him as their sole parent and guardian. This, they suggested, would provide added complications, but granted that these hurdles were safely negotiated, there remained the matter of ensuring, in advance, through the appropriate governmental channels in the West Indies that the applicant's parents or other relatives were in a position to give the children proper care, comfort and attention.

The final difficulty was the one on which many a hopeful plan foundered, money. One official put it this way.

"In such cases it must be clearly understood that the applicant must bear all the expenses incurred. In the case of small children we arrange for someone travelling out to the West Indies to take care of the children during the journey, for an agreed fee to be paid in advance, separate and distinct from the children's fare.

"There is one way, however, in which the applicant may bypass these various requirements; that is by taking the children out of the country himself. As their father and legal guardian he is free to take such action. Let me remind you once again that, whatever is done, must be done entirely at his own expense."

Afterwards I chatted with some of the members of staff about the many problems which demanded their attention. For them each day was several hours too short, and the more I heard, the more I realized how fearfully undermanned they were, to meet the heavy burdens imposed on them. Each week they met hundreds of new immigrants in the chaotic conditions of airport or rail terminal, with the attendant problems of baggage misplaced or stolen, children lost or strayed, newcomers flimsily clothed against the British climate and frequently without enough money to provide additional warm clothing or to support themselves until they could find employment. Sometimes, they encountered young women bewildered by the sudden discovery of pregnancy, with no assurance of any support from the young man with whom they had struck up the shipboard romance; or wives arrived with children and no sign of the husband and father they expected would be waiting for them.

"It can be rough," one of them said. "Just think of it. Anything from four to eight hundred immigrants at Waterloo Station on a cold night, and only one of us on the spot."

"Why only one of you?"

"Well, the truth is that we go primarily to meet the students for whose reception we are responsible, although, once on the spot, one sometimes has to lend a helping hand to others."

I offered the opinion that when a group of three or four hundred new arrivals observed that a few fellow travellers, the students, were singled out for special treatment, they were likely to believe that they were the victims of a kind of social ostracism, and the essential purpose of the Migrants' Services might thus be defeated. It seemed to me that though it was certainly necessary to give students every possible help towards settling into their new environment, it was equally important that the immigrant workers, generally less sophisticated than the students, be given a favourable impression of their first exposure to conditions in Britain. I suggested that some attempt be made to organize reception groups from among students and others already settled in Britain, who would volunteer to meet new arrivals at airports and rail terminals, and help them through some of their difficulties. Such groups could work either independently or in co-operation with one or other of the more familiar volunteer organizations such as the W.V.S. and the Salvation Army. This type of volunteer activity might provide useful experience for some of the bright young people of the hostels at Collingham Gardens and Hans Crescent who seemed over-supplied with leisure.

They told me of some other aspects of their work. They travelled around the country, especially to those cities and towns where groups of immigrants lived and worked, talking with civic and religious personalities and organizations, employers and employment agencies, addressing schools, seeking in every way to encourage harmony between the immigrants and the host community in which they now lived and worked.

"The work is harder on the spirit than on the feet," one said. "Sometimes liaison has to be done during one of those unhappy incidents which occasionally erupt as evidence of the disturbing depth of the fear and suspicion on which inter-racial disharmony so greedily feeds. At such times the going is really tough, especially when there seems to be some justification for the opinions expressed and the attitudes taken. In the quiet times we try to encourage the new citizens to enter boldly into the life of the community, but with little success. You see, most of them leave home and arrive in Britain with no clear image of themselves, no consciousness of their dignity or human worth; so when they are subjected to the pressure of prejudice and discrimination they are very likely to see themselves as others see them, to borrow the image of themselves, and, resenting it, to become equally prejudiced and bigoted as those who despise them and treat them shamefully. In such cases, any attempt we make at reconciliation is seen as a betrayal, especially as we can do little more than talk. Without the financial resources for starting any positive action programme, our talk must sound empty and meaningless to them."

"What do you mean by 'action programme'?" I asked.

"As we move around we see that a great deal needs to be done, to give the new citizens a sense of purpose beside the more simple essentials of food, clothes and shelter. They need to be encouraged to help improve their own conditions in terms of education, standards of hygiene, civic consciousness, etc. They must be encouraged to improve the image they have of themselves."

"Best of luck to you."

"Needs more than luck. Needs more of us and a few small miracles. A lot of our people leave home full of hope and trust in the people of Britain; soon after they arrive everything changes, and even those who achieve a measure of success do so at the cost of a great deal of spiritual bruising which embitters them. Yes, we need some miracles."

Mr Cosson arrived in London a few days later. I had sent him all the relevant information about his accommodation at the Redmonds, so he went directly to their house and later called at my office. Dressed in a smartly cut suit of brown tweeds, polished brown shoes, cream shirt and grey flecked maroon silk tie, he presented a picture of confidence and affluence, a far cry from the grey-clad sycophant I had met in the prison. I led him to one of the interview rooms, so that we could chat undisturbed.

"Well, here I am," he said. "Thanks a lot."

Smoothly shaved, his teeth white against his dark skin, he was smiling and relaxed as if he had not a care in the world, yet, for some reason which even now eludes me, I felt a gnawing dislike of him. We chatted awhile about nothing in particular, waiting for the word or gesture which leads into comfortable conversation. Then, "I remember you," he suddenly said.

I thought, 'Here it comes,' and mentally braced myself against whatever it was he might say.

"I've been trying to place you ever since the day you came up to see me, and at last I've got it. The Howard Hotel. Remember? During the Notting Hill thing when Mr Manley came over. I didn't place your name, but I remember your face. You were the one who didn't agree with the rest of them."

I hope he didn't notice any relief. Yes, I remembered the occasion, but I did not remember him as part of it. The Notting Hill thing as he called it, had caught many of us off guard by the suddenness of its eruption and the viciousness and depths of the interracial antipathy it exposed in a district where the various elements in the community seemed at least tolerant of each other. Furthermore, the black residents, leaderless and sadly inept, had in desperation sent an urgent appeal to the West Indian leader to come and speak up for them, in the hope that his political stature would earn for him and them a courteous hearing of their case, and result in an easing of their difficulties. Well, now he had arrived, and was sitting calm and assured among those who considered themselves the leaders among the immigrant community. They told him of their difficulties, describing in vivid and touching detail the numerous deliberate or subtle ways in which their persons and dignity were constantly assaulted. Now, with the veil crudely torn from the bland face of prejudice, they were being terrorized, even in their very homes. They wanted him, on their behalf, to remind the British people that, in spite of their black skins, they too were British, and had proved it through nearly three hundred years of close identity of language, culture, belief and thought; they hoped he would further remind the British people of their unstinted contribution, to the extent of the final sacrifice, during two world wars, and now all they wished for was the opportunity to work and live without fear of molestation or interference. On and on it went. Their complaints were true enough; there was no denying the facts; but there was something of defeat and acceptance in the very presentation of their difficulties, with never a hint of anything they themselves might attempt to do to arrest or alter the unhappy tide of events. They were deeply hurt and loquaciously angry, yet, unreasonably, or so it seemed to me, they expected him to achieve some effective results by restating the old relationships between Britain and her Caribbean territories, as if such a pitiful manoeuvre would somehow shame the British people into a friendlier, more tolerant attitude.

He sat there, the personification of dignity and wisdom, listening to them, his snowy hair adding emphasis to the majestic width of his forehead. Then he spoke, saying the things they expected of him, making the promises, giving the reassurances, and, hearing the easy, compelling rhetoric of the man, I was half-persuaded to believe. But I had lived in Britain a long time, and I knew that his arguments and protestations would receive short shrift. I rather suspected that he was aware of the danger that his plausible assurances might be taken too literally; with his long political experience and close association with British policies, he could not truly believe that his presence would dramatically resolve the racial disharmony. He must know that, in the street, he would be merely another black face, another object for disrespect, another potential target for the bottle or brick, another 'rabble-rouser' to be roughhandled by the police.

When he had said his piece and duly received the enthusiastic plaudits of his hearers, I asked his permission to speak. I reminded him that his professional and political interests would make it impossible for him to spend more than a few days in Britain, in spite of his emotional involvement in the situation. He would, as promised, visit the cities and towns where "his people were in trouble," and I agreed that his presence would prove stimulating and encouraging to them. But after a few days he'd be forced to return to the West Indies to deal with matters more immediately important to his political career. It seemed to me that throughout

E. R. BRAITHWAITE

all their protestations, none of those present had indicated any recognition of responsibility, on the part of the black residents in Britain, for even a small part of the trouble. I told him that those who had been exhorting him to representative action on their behalf did not really represent the thousands for whom they claimed to speak; in fact, they hardly knew them or had anything more than the vaguest contact with them. The current state of frightening disorder had temporarily shocked and frightened them, but I felt safe in prophesying that as soon as the situation eased a bit, they would quickly return to their separate personal pursuits until the next rash of incidents threw them once again into agitated association. I made the suggestion that he urge them to recognize their own responsibility in the matter. Racial discrimination in Britain was not an overnight phenomenon, and it was pitiable that there still could be found no effective representative group of West Indians in Britain who could honestly claim the right to speak or act on behalf of the rank and file in time of crisis. They were on the spot, they were familiar with the circumstances, and they should be able to speak with a clearer knowledge of what action would best and most speedily resolve the situation. Many of them were easily and fluently articulate or otherwise gifted; they should put some of their talents to work to help raise the standards of those less equipped than themselves. Without doubt, he represented the 'father figure', but he should put first things first with some plain talk to those who so obviously were prepared to sit back and let him attempt to solve their problems.

He received my words in silence; the others angrily interrupted me while I was speaking, and were even more vociferous at the end. But I didn't give a damn about their abuse. However, it was clear that he had no intention of committing himself by commenting on anything I had said, so I left them. As I approached the door of the hotel, I was intercepted by a tall, handsome woman.

"Mr Braithwaite," she said, "I am Mrs Manley."

We shook hands.

"I am grateful to you for the things you just said to my husband."

That was all, and we parted before I had really seen her to remember; except her voice, deep and round, but trembling with more than a hint of anxiety . . .

Yes, I remembered that occasion although I could not recall Mr Cosson's face as a piece of the group.

"Those buggers let me down," he went on. "That time at Notting Hill, Mr Manley said that anybody who got into trouble with the police and suchlike, would be looked after, you know, they'd be represented or, if they were fined, those would be paid. Well, I was in a car with some fellows one night and the police stopped us. We had a few things in the car, you know, to defend ourselves in case of anything, but the police ran us in and charged us with carrying offensive weapons. We were fined and we had to pay it ourselves. Didn't see one of those big shots who promised to do so much."

I said nothing. A lot of wild, irresponsible promises had been scattered around at the time, and there had been a great deal of misunderstanding because the promises had been taken too literally.

"Anyway, not to worry," he said, laughing. "Thanks for helping out with this thing." He meant his ticket of leave.

"Glad to do it. The children will be happy to see you."

"I know; I'm thinking of what to tell them."

"They've already been told that you were away ill, so I suppose it won't hurt if you follow the same line."

"I wasn't thinking about that." He waved his hand airily. "Now they'll want to know when they can come home with me."

"You mean to British Guiana?"

"No, I mean here, London. They'll want me to take them from that Home."

"Well, what plans do you have for them?"

"I've been figuring it out," he continued. "I could start a shop somewhere else and rent a flat for me and the children; could always get somebody to come in and keep an eye on them." He laughed again, probably enjoying some private joke. "This time I'm taking no chances."

He was silent for a few moments, as if mentally determining how much he should say to me. "Last time one of them shopped me, but it won't happen again. I've learned a few things inside. When I come out it's going to be different, you can bet on that."

I suddenly had an idea about Mr Cosson, and thought I'd test it. "When you're out, we'd be happy to do whatever we can to help you find a job . . . "

He interrupted me. "Oh, don't worry about that. I know where I can put my hand on some money to make a start. I'll be all right. You know what they say, 'If you can't be good, be careful.'"

Yes, I was right. He had no intention of seeking honest employment. His term of imprisonment had not produced a change of heart, but merely a determination to be more careful, at least, until next time. The more I saw and heard of Mr Cosson, the less I liked him.

"May I make a suggestion, Mr Cosson." My voice and manner were stiff and formal, because I disliked the way in which, by his attitude as well as the things he said, it seemed I was being made a kind of conspirator in his schemes.

"Sure, why not?"

"I think it would be the best thing for you and the children if they remained where they are until you have been freed and settled into whatever it is you wish to do. Meanwhile you could write them as often as possible, and visit them when you are able."

"Yes," he agreed, too quickly. "You're right; that would be the best thing to do."

He left soon after, taking with him, as gifts for the children, some books and toys from a collection kept at the office for exactly that purpose.

Next morning I had a telephone call from the Matron at Falconbridge; Mr Cosson had appeared as planned; the children were somewhat shy with him at first, but eventually they had got along quite well. Except for the eldest girl; her father's visit seemed to have unsettled her and Matron had heard her crying during the night and went in to her. Things were now back to normal. I got the impression that Matron would be happier if Mr Cosson's visits were even fewer.

I did not see Mr Cosson again; he telephoned me from the railway station just before getting his train back North, to express his thanks again for everything which had been done for him. When I visited the Redmonds to pay them for Mr Cosson's board and accommodation, they expressed their complete satisfaction and delight with him; they had found him thoughtful, courteous and a delightful companion and were willing to accommodate him on any future occasion. I was very pleased to hear all this, but inwardly hoped that there would be no repeat occasion. In the report I submitted on the case and Mr Cosson's visit, I expressed the opinion that there seemed little likelihood of any change in the circumstances of the Cosson children; the best that could be hoped for was that Mr Cosson would keep in touch with them.

Chapter *Eight*

T WO DAYS LATER THE Supervisor called me to her office.

"Trouble," she said, as I came in.

"Roddy Williams?"

"I'm afraid so."

"What's the latest development?"

"Middlesex still won't play. Just as I feared, the situation does not look very hopeful. It's the old argument about creating a precedent which they believe will adversely affect their programme."

"Do they appreciate that this is the only chance we have had, so far, to place the boy in an ordinary home?"

"Oh yes, they are in possession of all the relevant information on him, but I suppose there is some justification for their arguments."

I suppose she was right, but I had not yet acquired the technique of maintaining a certain distance from each case, the better to view it with clarity and objectivity.

"Suppose we suggest to Middlesex that they find a family willing to accept their terms and provide a home for him?" I could not quite keep the bitterness and disappointment out of my voice.

"No, that would never do," she replied, in her usual careful, level tone. "We must press on with it until they either give in or finally commit themselves to the unpleasantness of refusal. Don't forget, from their point of view, an equally important matter of principle is involved. However, let's not resign ourselves to defeat while the battle is still joined; we've still a few more strings to pull in high places."

Somehow I did not feel disposed to share her lightheartedness. "So what do I say to the Tamerlanes?"

"Why say anything to them about it until we know something definite one way or another? I'd be inclined to let things go along as they are now for a while. We'll soon know what the final word is, but, don't forget, we're being supported at very high level. And don't worry too much," she advised.

I went out to the Tamerlanes' home on Saturday afternoon, having heard from the Matron at Franmere that Roddy would be spending the afternoon with them. They were all in the backyard, John and Ella sunning themselves in deck-chairs while the children romped with the dog on the grass between bouts on the swing. I was soon in the thick of being hugged and kissed as June, Jackie and Roddy simultaneously tried to bring me up to date on everything they had done, each one screaming "Uncle Ricky" in my ears. Warm, frantic and wonderful. Roddy fitted into it all so naturally, it seemed unthinkable that anything could happen to interfere with this heaven-sent chance. I finally disengaged myself from the children and sat on the grass beside the parents.

"We've a surprise for him," Ella whispered to me. "Matron agreed that if everything went well we could keep him over the weekend and take him back on Sunday night or early Monday morning." Her delight in the seeming success of the venture radiated from her face.

"That's good." But my worry must have got through to them.

"Has anything happened?" John asked.

As the Supervisor had advised, there was no sense in making them uneasy. "Don't get alarmed. I just want to remind you that we're still waiting for the green light from Middlesex, and where bureaucracy is concerned anything can happen."

"Is that all?" said Ella, relieved. "For a moment you sounded like the voice of doom. Anyway I've some news that might cheer you up. Your friend Miss Keriham is coming to tea."

John pointed to the oak-tree. The three children had climbed out along the lowest branch and were hanging upside down by their knees several feet above the ground. Ella instantly tried to rise, but John restrained her.

"Leave them alone," he said, although his voice betrayed his concern. As we watched, one by one they righted themselves and climbed down to the ground. Although smaller than the girls, Roddy seemed well able to match their tomboy exploits.

"Come on, everybody, time to get washed," Ella called, masking her relief with a flurry of domestic activity. The girls scampered off upstairs, and Ella busied herself laying the table for tea, while John and I sat idly in the sitting-room.

"Somehow I've got the feeling you're holding something back from us," he began. "You seem to be anticipating some difficulty we know nothing about."

"No, not really. We're still working on the Middlesex people and there is no way of knowing how it will be. The boy seems so completely at his ease here, it would be a shame if we can't go through with the plan."

"And what about the girls, not to mention Ella and me? They've already made up their minds about him. How can we tell them he couldn't come to live with us? Would it help if I wrote to the Middlesex people?"

"There's no need for that just yet, anyway. I suppose I'm worrying unnecessarily and communicating my fears to you. Let's just forget about it until we have some definite news."

There was a ring on the doorbell and John answered, returning with Olga. As usual she was smartly though simply dressed. At the sound of her voice Ella came from the dining-room and I introduced Olga to them. Ella returned to her chores, but soon the children descended upon us and became more excited with Olga, who had to be taken on a tour of the house and backyard, hand in hand with Roddy, who thus masterfully underlined his relationship to Auntie Olga.

Tea was a happy though somewhat noisy affair, but much of the time I watched the two women, who, though going through all the motions of relaxed friendliness, seemed to be carefully feeling their way around and towards each other. Ella had changed into a bright gingham dress of tiny black and white squares, set off by a wide belt of red leather drawn tightly at the waist to emphasize her full yet girlish figure. Her thick brown hair framed her face in loose, soft curls, but the large grey eyes above the high cheekbones indicated maturity and resolve which was further supported by her dimpled yet aggressive-looking chin. Against the background of her home and family her naturalness and assurance were easily equal to the smooth elegance with which Olga managed to invest the simplest gesture, and I marvelled at the odd turn of events which had brought them together.

Roddy was the centre-piece of the group and seemed to know it, yet, so well had he been taught at Franmere, that though he was literally bubbling with the excitement of his first really family tea-party, each request began with "please may I have," and there was a sweet, bright-eyed "thank you" when helped; Ella beamed at this, very much as if she had been responsible for it, while the girls tried to outbid each other waiting on him. After tea John, Olga and I were pushed into the sitting-room to talk while the others cleared away and washed up.

I rode back to London in Olga's car.

"Looks as if your worries about Roddy are over," she said. "He seems to have fitted in very well with the Tamerlanes."

"I'm not too sure. There's one large fly in the ointment, but we're working on it."

I told her about our difficulties with Middlesex, and the cause of them; after all, she was as involved with Roddy as were the rest of us, so there was no point in being secretive on that point. As we drove she questioned me on ways and means of circumventing that difficulty, hinting rather broadly at the possibility that some 'interested party' might be willing to contribute the difference between the Middlesex rate and the amount agreed on by the Tamerlanes. I explained why such an arrangement was impracticable and expressed the view that there were so many pressures built into the situation that eventually Middlesex would probably capitulate.

"I'll be keeping my fingers crossed for you," she said. "You know, I sort of have the feeling Mrs Tamerlane is not too keen on me seeing the boy."

"Why do you say that? Has she said or done something?"

"No, it's just a feeling I have."

In the silence that followed I became aware of the late afternoon traffic rushing about us, and the sounds which somehow had not invaded the little sanctuary in which we were smoothly rolling, as Olga weaved easily along, completely familiar with the puzzling complexities of London's streets. Her red-gloved hands rested lightly on the wheel, in pleasing contrast to the tanned skin of her forearms and the pale shiny linen suit she wore. Now and then one hand would fall lightly on to the gear lever, and the gear change would be effortlessly made.

"Right now, right this minute, I'd give up a hell of a lot just to have a boy like that. No, not any boy, just him."

She said this very quietly, but with such feeling that I wished it were possible for her to do just that. A funny remark popped into my head, but I decided against saying it, it would have been too much like an intrusion on something very private.

We drove through the City to Liverpool Street Station where I could take a train for Ilford.

"I hope you won't let anything keep you from seeing him whenever you can," I said, as I was leaving her.

"You mean the Tamerlanes? Not unless she comes right out and tells me I'm not welcome, and I have an idea she's too well bred to do that." The smile was back on her face and the laughter in her voice.

Mrs Bentham called to see me on Monday. When the telephone operator mentioned the name of my visitor I had visions of further difficulties in the Bentham household, and went downstairs mentally preparing myself to meet whatever it might be. She was standing near the operator's cabinet, looking taller and lovelier than I had remembered her, probably because of the extra inches from the high stiletto heels of her neat black pumps, and the lipstick. She wore a one-piece costume of dark blue, light-weight wool, which hugged her comely frame affectionately, and as I led her to one of the interview rooms I noticed how easily, effortlessly she moved, like a professional dancer, swinging smoothly from the hip in a continuous blending of controlled musculature and accommodating cloth. Only big women with good figures are able to achieve that kind of movement.

As soon as we were seated she spoke, as if impatient to tell it quickly before the fermented pleasure exploded within her.

"We've got a house." Her eyes were literally aglow in her face. "Jim's firm has transferred him to Harlow where they're doing a lot of building, and they helped him to find a house."

"Congratulations," I said, "are you renting it?"

They were buying it, she explained. They had paid the deposit and would be able to move in soon. The people at Jim's firm were helping with the arrangements, and Jim would be able to pay so much each week. She had been down to see it last weekend, and quite obviously she was thrilled with it.

"I think you need a drink," I said, "but you'll have to settle for a cigarette." I offered her one, and lit it.

"When we move down you must come and see it," she went on, the cigarette held lightly in her large, firmly-shaped hands which were cupped together on the table. My mother used to sit like that when anything pleased or excited her, her hands at rest as if patiently waiting for the excitement in the rest of her to work itself out, so they could resume their careful, considered activities.

She described the house. It was new, with lots of cupboard space, so that there was no need to buy wardrobes and things like that. It had three bedrooms, two big ones and a little one which, she said, would be wonderful for the baby.

"Sounds very comfortable," I said.

It had a little garden in front, for roses, and a back garden where Jim would be able to plant tomatoes and other things. And the neighbours seemed to be very nice. One had been hanging clothes on her line while they were in the backyard and they had got to talking, and she had invited them in for a cup of tea. It was all so different from the other place.

I had the feeling she'd soon run out of breath.

"Any news from the baby's mother?"

"Oh, her? Like I told Jim right from the first, we won't hear another word from her. She was glad to dump the child and be off, probably back to her old habits again."

"I think it might be advisable for Mr Bentham to make inquiries about adopting the child legally," I suggested, "against the chance that she might suddenly reappear one day to claim the child. If he can prove that she has left the child in his care it might not be difficult for him to adopt her; then the mother could not come back to claim her. I'm not familiar with the processes involved, but a lawyer would be able to advise him."

"That's been worrying me, I must tell you. As soon as Jim comes in tonight I'll tell him. I'm not going to let her take it away now, not after all the trouble she's caused with Jim and me."

"Where have you left her?"

"With a friend in Aldgate. I didn't take her to the nursery today because I'm having the day off from work. When we go to Harlow Jim says I must stay at home and look after the baby. I'll like that. He's earning good money, so there's no need for me to go out to work. You should see her now, big and lovely as anything, and so

cute! You know, I wish she were really Jim's. Still, she's ours now—
but I wish we could have one of our very own."

"You never know, anything can happen," I said. An idea had
suddenly come to me.

"Sure, with a little help." The mischief twinkled in her eyes.

Impulsively I put it to her. "How would you like to take care of
two babies instead of one?"

"Oh, ho! What have you been up to?" she teased.

"Nothing yet, but there's a little boy who needs a home and I
think you would make him a wonderful mother."

"Tell me about him."

It was now nearly twelve-thirty.

"Why not let's have lunch together and we could talk about it?"

"You and me?"

"Of course, unless you wouldn't care to eat with me."

"You're joking. Of course I'd love to."

We went to a small, rather old-fashioned restaurant nearby, generally frequented by local office staff. We were the only black couple
there and attracted some attention. Mrs Bentham took it well in her
stride. As we ate: "I bet they think we're married," she whispered, her
eyes glinting with mischief. "Now tell me about your little boy."

I told her about Roddy, omitting any mention of the Tamerlanes, but explained that certain plans were in hand which might
or might not finally work out.

"What would you like me to do?" she asked.

"Nothing, at least not yet. If the thing I'm working on now fiz-
zles out I'll let you know, but I must confess that I felt this was too
good an opportunity to miss, just in case I need it."

"Poor little thing," she sympathized. "For myself I wouldn't
hesitate a moment about accepting him, but I don't know how Jim

would feel about it. Men are funny about such things. But, what with one thing and another," she grinned, "I don't suppose he'd make too much noise. Shall I mention it to him?"

"No, I'd rather you didn't. We'll leave it like this for a while and if necessary I'll let you know. But keep your fingers crossed for me."

We chatted about other things, chiefly about the new house. It was one big wonderful adventure for her; at long last she could, as she put it, 'lock her own front door'. She planned to go shopping for curtains, furniture, dishes, all the things a housewife needs, and, listening to her, I knew she'd turn the new house into a comfortable home, less with the new furnishings than with her own effervescent personality.

I plunged headlong into a sticky situation. A couple appeared at my office one day. When I went down to them I saw a young but hard-looking brunette with jet black hair and straight eyebrows which met above her nose. Not the sort to mess about with tweezers, I thought. Smartly dressed, but with too much shiny jewellery. With her was a thin, very black man, whom I guessed was an African, probably Sudanese. He was handsome in a rather fierce way, and neatly dressed.

"I'm Martin's mother," the woman said.

"Whose mother?"

"Martin Devonish. Remember? You sent some letters to me."

Then I remembered. Since I'd taken over the case seven weeks ago I had been trying to locate her by writing to both the addresses at which she had been known to reside during recent months. The letters had not been returned, so I assumed that she had received them, but there had been no reply from her.

"I'm glad to meet you at last, Miss Devonish. My name is Braithwaite."

"This is Mr Agumsah," she said, "I'm called Mrs Agumsah."

I looked at her hands but no wedding ring; that's why she 'was called' Mrs Agumsah.

"We'd like to take Martin out of the Home."

Just like that, and I was pleased to hear it. If a few more prodigal parents would turn up and say, "I'd like to take my child out of the Home," I might soon have to return to teaching. Suddenly it was a nice, warm, sunny day.

"If you'll both wait here," I said, showing them into one of the interview rooms, "I'll get the case folder and be with you in a moment."

The case folder did not present a very flattering picture of Miss Devonish, otherwise known as Mrs Agumsah. It stated that three years ago the child had been brought to the Council's attention by the N.S.P.C.C., one of whose officers had found him alone and crying in a dirty, unheated room; a neighbour had reported hearing the child crying for hours. An African had later appeared and said that the child's mother, with whom he had been living, had that morning disappeared and he was unable to care for the child; he had left it in the unheated room while he went to search for the mother. The child had been taken into care, but all attempts at tracing the mother had failed. The African, Mr Agumsah, had insisted that though he had been living with the mother he was not the baby's father. The child's name and that of the mother were supplied by him. The child had been taken to Campden Hill residential nursery where Mr Agumsah visited it at irregular intervals during the first year of its stay there.

Suddenly during his second year, Miss Devonish had appeared one Sunday with Mr Agumsah, had brought gifts for the baby, but had refused to give her address or indicate when next she would visit; irregular and widely spaced visits by the mother had continued, but the Welfare Officer in charge was unable to see her because it was never known when she would appear. The Matron at Campden Hill had tried to get her address from Mr Agumsah, but he had refused to co-operate.

On the baby boy's third birthday he had appeared in a car with new clothing for him and had requested permission to take him for a ride in the car, but Matron had refused to allow this, because, on his own admission, he was not related to the child. He had become angry and abusive, and since then, though he continued to visit, his attitude to the Nursery staff was no longer friendly.

About nine months ago the Council had assumed the Rights and Privileges of Parenthood over the child, as a precautionary measure, in the event of the child becoming ill, or any other circumstance developing which would require an immediate decision to be taken; the mother's infrequent and unexpected visits made it impossible to rely on her availability for parental consent in an emergency.

Soon after this measure was taken the mother appeared, again with Mr Agumsah. They wanted to take the child out into the town, but were prevented by Matron, who insisted that they could not be allowed to take him beyond the nursery grounds; if the mother wished for greater freedom of action she would need to apply for revocation of the order which had granted the rights and privileges to the Council. She had again disappeared without trace.

I had added notes in the case folder referring to each occasion which I had written to her.

The report from the Nursery showed that the little boy had recently had a tonsilectomy, was in excellent health, intelligent and cheerful. He knew Mr Agumsah, whom he called 'Daddy' and was delighted whenever he visited him. He called Miss Devonish 'Mummy' on her insistence, but was shy of her, and was not easily persuaded to go to her.

I knew the contents of the case folder nearly verbatim, so often had I studied it. Now here was Martin's mother wanting her child.

"I've recently taken over Martin's case, Mrs Agumsah, but all that I know of it I have either read in the case sheet or been told by the Welfare Officer who first dealt with it. I've chatted with the Matron on a few occasions in an attempt to get in touch with you. I'd like to hear your story about this whole business however. Why did you abandon the child in the first place?"

"Abandon?" her voice was a screech of alarm. "What do you mean abandon? Who said I abandoned him?"

"According to the case records you walked out of the house and left him with Mr Agumsah."

"Ali, did you tell them that?" She turned on him like a vengeful harpy.

"I told the people I do not know where you go." He chose each word carefully, without seeming to care about her anger.

"I didn't abandon him. I left the house to go to the shops and I fell down in the street; I'd been sick with my chest. Somebody called an ambulance and they took me to hospital. They said I had pleurisy. I was sick for weeks. And the hospital sent me away for convalescence."

"Didn't you tell them about the baby?"

"I thought the baby would be all right with Ali, so I didn't worry. Only afterwards he told me they had put him in the Home. While I was away he had to give up the flat we had and he went to stay with one of his friends. I've been bunking with a girl friend, so I thought it best to let him stay in the Home till we could find somewhere to have him with us."

Something was missing in her story. It had taken her more than three years to reach this point, and I had the feeling that perhaps Mr Agumsah had more to do with her decision than was apparent. He sat there, calm, but watchful, as if witnessing the fact that she kept a promise. In my short experience of the job, I had been learning some hard lessons, one of which was that parents behave in the oddest ways, and the fact that a child had been left to the Council's care might have little bearing on the parents' love for it. An abandoned child was always the object of pity and was sure of help, either private or public. What about abandoned parents, those tragic figures who are sometimes literally pressured into the decision of abandoning a child or children whom they love, choosing that drastic way of ensuring that it received the food, clothing and shelter which they could no longer provide? For many excellent reasons, County Councils make it difficult for a mother deliberately and willingly to place her child in their care. Here was a mother who wanted her child, this was the end result I was paid to achieve, and here it was being handed to me on a platter. But I ought to learn the full story.

"Do you know, Mrs Agumsah, that the Council now exercises the rights of a parent over your child?"

"I don't know anything about that. All I know is that he's my baby and we want him with us. We've now got a nice place where we can have him and we want him out of that Home."

"Have you been to see the Matron at Campden Hill?"

"We were there yesterday and she said we couldn't have the child till the people at County Hall said we could. She doesn't like me, that woman. She and Ali had a hell of a row. Excuse me."

"Why did Mr Agumsah quarrel with her?"

This brought him suddenly out of his shell.

"I did not make quarrel with that woman. She made quarrel with me. I tell I want to take Martin. She say, 'No, no'. She want to keep baby for herself, that woman. I tell so."

Suddenly he laughed, a wicked-sounding chuckle which temporarily dispersed the stern watchfulness from his eyes.

"I tell," he went on, "if she love baby so much maybe I make baby with her, but I take Martin. I think she make trouble, that woman."

As quickly as it had appeared the laughter vanished, leaving the face once more stern and remote. They evidently had run into some difficulties with the Matron. I'd better check that before going any further, and do it while they were present to avoid any suggestion of connivance. I picked up the telephone and asked to be connected with the Campden Hill Nursery. The Matron answered and I told her that Miss Devonish was with me requesting that she be allowed to have Martin.

The best I can say is that the Matron was not enthusiastic about Miss Devonish. Miss Richardson, the child's house mother had informed her of Miss Devonish's visit the previous day and the extremely rude things which had been said to her by Miss Devonish's friend. Furthermore, the child had become very upset when his mother tried to take him away. Matron explained that Miss Richardson was very attached to Martin as she had cared for him from the moment he had been brought to the nursery, and she was very upset at the thought of his being once again exposed to neglect and mistreatment.

As she spoke I could hear the anger taking hold in her voice, then:

"Personally, I do not trust the woman; if she could heartlessly abandon her child and stay away from him until now, except for a few fleeting visits, there's no guarantee that she won't abandon him again. As for the man with whom she is associating, he is not Martin's father, and there's no reason to suppose that she will remain with him for any length of time. We cannot let the child go to them until we are quite satisfied that he will be well cared for and safe. I have my doubts about that woman's way of life."

"How is Martin now?"

"He was a bit upset after his mother's visit, but he's quite settled down again. Miss Richardson takes care of him wonderfully well."

Well, there it was. While I was telephoning my visitors were watching me closely and listening hard; probably they could guess that Matron was not overly keen. For myself I favoured the view that a far from perfect parent in a mediocre home is better for a child than an excellent institution with wonderful staff. I could not concern myself with Mrs Agumsah's morals, or whether she was saint or sinner. And Mr Agumsah, just where did he fit into all this? I asked him.

"Where do you come into this?"

"I'm Martin's father."

"According to the file you are not."

"But I am."

"Yes, he is," the woman agreed. Two against one.

"Why did you not say so long ago? According to the records Martin's father is unknown."

"He's Martin's father. I should know," she insisted.

Of course you should, I thought. Maybe he was, his regular visits to the child seemed to indicate more than casual interest. Until now I had not even thought that the child was of mixed parentage. The case folder did not mention it, for a change.

Then a thought struck me and I immediately threw it at him. "As the father you might be expected to contribute to his maintenance for the time he is at Campden Hill."

"I am telling you I am the father."

I studied that one. He was telling me, but perhaps in another place he would deny it. I did not pursue the matter; there were others who were better qualified to deal with that.

"You said you had found accommodation, Mrs Agumsah?"

"Yes, we've got a nice place near Tower Bridge, and I can get a job at the mattress factory. But I'd stay at home for a week or two at first, to let Martin get accustomed to me, before going out to work."

All very plausible. And the inescapable fact was that she was the child's mother and wanted him.

"I want my baby." The woman burst into tears. I don't know how sincere she was; I could never know that. These difficult cases had been dumped in my lap and it was up to me to clear them up; the woman had come here, of her own free will, so it seemed, wanting to take her child into her own care. I felt that it was my business to do something about it.

"Mrs Agumsah, before taking any further action I'd like to see the place where you plan to live with Martin."

"Okay, you can come with us now if you like. We've got a car outside, we can take you there and bring you back."

I went with them to an old grimy house near Tower Bridge, up two flights of stairs to a room, simply furnished, the type with which I had become very familiar since starting this job. A large double bed, table, four straight chairs and a gas-ring on a shelf in one corner. The floor was covered with linoleum. A wide clothes closet was built into one wall. Clean. And bright with sunlight through a wide, uncurtained window.

"Where will you put the child?"

She reached under the bed and pulled out a small folding bed, and a screen of wooden framework and gaily patterned cretonne panels.

"We can set this up each evening," she explained. She then showed me where, a short distance along the corridor, there were bathroom and toilet facilities which they shared with two other roomers on the same floor. Simple, unpretentious, not too comfortable, but I knew of many families of four or more housed in as much space or even less.

"What happens to him when you begin work?" I asked her.

"I can put him in a day nursery and collect him each evening." She had evidently given the matter some thought; probably, between them they had carefully worked it out. Well, why not. Other parents were doing the same thing. It was her child.

"Why not sit down?" he invited. They both sat on the bed.

"Look here, both of you," I was making my decision as I went along. "I want to help you. If one judges by the history of this case, you have not done much to encourage trust. As things are it would be well within our rights to keep the child at Campden Hill, until you make formal application to the courts to have the Council's rights rescinded. However, I am willing to take a chance on you. I will have Martin turned over to you, but I will come regularly to check that he is comfortable and happy; at the least sign of neglect he will be returned to the Home."

Mrs Agumsah beamed with pleasure and relief. The African merely grinned. If they were merely putting on an act, then so consummate was their performance that it deserved to succeed. They asked if they could have Martin straight away.

"Not today," I said, "because I'll have to notify Matron of my decision. And the child will need to be medically examined and cleared before he is released to you."

They drove me back to my office, and I put through a call to Campden Hill. Matron was not available, so I asked to be connected with Miss Richardson; I told her what I planned to do.

"But you can't. You can't hand him over to those awful people." She sounded very agitated. I repeated that Martin's mother would call for him soon after noon the following day—that should allow enough time for all the formalities to be completed.

"But he's in the Council's Care and Protection." She made the words sound special and capitalized. "We can't let him go without special permission."

"I'll take the responsibility for that, Miss Richardson." She seemed to be taking it rather personally, so I took this tougher line. Little did I know just how much responsibility I was so casually undertaking.

"I'll have to tell Matron."

"Yes, of course. I tried to tell her myself, but couldn't reach her. Tell her that Martin's parents will be there tomorrow."

I suddenly had the misgiving that I might have acted too precipitately, so I went to the Chief's office to let her know what I had done; a bit late, but never mind. Neither she nor Miss Whitney was in, so, having gone so far with the matter, I'd have to see it through.

Next day was Saturday, but in the afternoon I went to the room near Tower Hill to check on progress. What I saw gave me a wonderful feeling of satisfaction and encouragement. Through the open door I saw Mr Agumsah lying on his back on the floor, with a lovely child astride his chest, bouncing up and down and squealing with merriment. He was fair-skinned, with large dark eyes and very dark hair which hung from his head in long glossy curls. On his head was a green ribbon tied in a big bow adding an attractive dash of colour. He sat still as I appeared and regarded me shyly. Then Mr Agumsah, looked around and said:

"Come in. This is my Martin."

Very nice, except for the green ribbon. As I drew nearer the boy leaned down and hugged his father, for protection, I thought.

"Mrs Agumsah in?"

"No, she's out shopping. Will be back soon."

He sat up, still keeping the shy child close to him, cooing soft nothings to him meanwhile. Mrs Agumsah soon appeared, laden with groceries.

"Was everything okay at the Home?" I asked them.

"It wasn't bad. Martin cried a bit at first, but he was soon all right. Well, you can see for yourself."

Yes, I saw for myself, but I told her I would be dropping around from time to time and, when she decided to return to work, I'd like to know where the child would be placed . . . .

The storm broke over my head on Monday morning. Hardly had I entered my office when my telephone rang and the crisp voice of the Chief called me to her office. Sitting straight behind her desk, she shot at me:

"I have heard from Campden Hill of your extremely high-handed action in the Devonish case. Without any authority what-soever you have undertaken to remove a child from the Council's care and deliver it to persons of whom the little that is known could not reasonably be quoted to their advantage. I want to make it clear, here and now, that your conduct in this matter will, in all probability, have very serious consequences for you; furthermore, because you saw fit to act without reference to me, I hope you will appreciate that you have placed yourself outside the influence of any protection I would otherwise have extended to you as a member of this staff. Before you leave your office this morning you will please prepare a full report on this matter to be attached to my own report to County Hall."

Gradually it was getting to me; there was more to it than just that. I stood where I was, just inside the door.

"You came to this office without any formal training in this work, and you have completely overstepped your terms of reference." She stopped; probably she was finding it difficult to control the things within her which were clamouring to be said. "Well, have you anything to say?"

My surprise had now given way to a cold, incisive anger. At such times the damnedest things pop into my head.

"Secondly," I replied, "a full report on the case is in that tray there on your desk, where it has been since Saturday, and, firstly, my terms of reference clearly allow me to do everything I can to resolve the hard-core cases, among which the Devonish case has been included. It seems to me that you have already made up your mind purely on whatever you have heard from persons at Campden Hill, therefore it would be pointless for me to say anything other than what is already in my report."

With that I bade her good morning and returned to my office, a prey to a sudden spate of misgivings. Perhaps, after all, I had fallen for a lot of sentimental nonsense from the Agumsahs . . . Yet, was not the sight of that little family, united and happy, sufficient justification? I sat at my desk, unable to concentrate on the work which needed attention. Suppose anything had happened to the child over the weekend. Suppose, suppose . . . I hurried downstairs and, half-running, rushed to the nearest taxi-stand and got a taxi for Tower Bridge.

Well, I need not have worried. I could hear their laughter as I ran up the steps. I knocked and Mrs Agumsah let me in; she and Martin were at breakfast.

"Ali goes to work very early, so we didn't hurry to get up." She wore a woollen dressing-gown over pyjamas, and the little boy was in a warm, fleecy combination garment.

"Everything okay?" I asked, trying to hide the fact that I felt rather foolish to be spying on her in this absurd way; she was kindness itself and gave no hint that she resented my intrusion.

"Yes, just fine." Then suddenly, "They won't try to come and take him from me, will they?"

"Nonsense, Mrs Agumsah. Nobody can take him away as long as you take good care of him."

She smiled in relief. When I left them I felt more than relief; I felt strong and ready to defend my decision, precipitate and arbitrary though it might seem. If the Council wanted these cases cleared up, they'd have to go along with me, red tape or no red tape. Whatever the Chief might say in her report, somebody would have to ask me some questions, and I had a few good answers ready and waiting.

Two mornings later the Chief rang me.

"I would like you to come to my office immediately, Mr Braithwaite." The peremptory tone spelled further trouble. She could hardly wait to tell me: "Miss Devonish, or whatever she calls herself, has disappeared again, this time taking the child with her." No anger in her voice now; the flat I-told-you-so statement, with the faintest hint of vindication for her own opinion of the woman. Or was it her own opinion?

"When did this happen?"

"Last night, I suppose. Miss Richardson came to see me yesterday and together we went to the address you supplied in your report. Someone in the house told us that the woman was out. We went back again later in the evening and discovered that she had paid her rent and gone, taking the child with her. According to the landlady, they put their stuff in a car and drove off, without leaving any forwarding address."

"Why did you take Miss Richardson?"

"Because she knows the child and would have been better able to judge if it were being properly cared for. Well, just as I said, the woman is completely unreliable."

"I think you frightened her away, you and Miss Richardson."

"That could hardly be true; we didn't see her."

"She probably saw you. What happens now?"

"You will be expected to find her and return the child to the Council's care."

If I had remained another moment with her I might have said things later to be regretted. I went to my office and carefully looked through the files, to try to find something that would give me a clue to her whereabouts. I was sure, or very nearly sure, that somehow Miss Richardson had been responsible for the woman's flight. The only clue I had was her remark about working at the mattress factory. I went there but the personnel officer had no news of her. I went back to see her landlady, hoping that either she or Mr Agumsah might have returned for some reason or other. Another blank. I could think of nothing else to do. Perhaps, after all, I was wrong to trust her.

Early next morning the man telephoned. He came immediately to the point.

"Why you send woman to take baby?"

I hastily assured him that there was no intention to take Martin away from them; the visitors had merely called to see how the child was getting along.

"That woman not come to take baby?"

"No, of course not, believe me." No answer, maybe he was making up his mind. I said: "Mr Agumsah, I trusted you when I let you take the boy home. I think you should trust me when I say he will not be taken from you."

"Okay, I trust you."

"Where are they, Mrs Agumsah and Martin?"

"In Brixton." He gave me the address. "She scared they take baby away."

"Don't worry. I'll go to see her and explain." I felt a little weak with relief. I'd get over there to see her as quickly as possible; but it might be a good idea to take someone else with me, so that someone less involved would be able to view the situation.

Ruth Martindale was busy at her desk nearby; I'd always found her helpful, sympathetic and rather more progressive in her outlook than most of the others. I gave her a quick rundown on the case and asked her if she could come with me to Brixton to visit Mrs Agumsah. She agreed.

It was a ground floor room in a small, two-storeyed, semidetached house, which looked like any of the hundreds of its neighbours in the narrow streets of Brixton. I knocked. A curtain twitched behind the window which overlooked the street, then the door opened. Before she could say anything I spoke.

"I'm very annoyed with you, Mrs Agumsah; running off like this without letting me know where you were. I told you that either I or one of my colleagues would have to visit you for a while. Why did you do it?"

"Won't you come in, Mr Braithwaite?" She looked inquiringly at Miss Martindale.

"Miss Martindale is a Welfare Officer. She came with me to see Martin."

"Okay, come in."

The room was somewhat bigger than that at Tower Bridge. Martin was on the floor playing with several clockwork replicas of automobiles. We sat down.

"Well, why did you disappear?"

Her face looked haggard with the strain of worry.

"It's that woman from the Home. I'd been shopping in the market with Martin, and while I was coming up the street I saw her and another woman stop at the house in a car; then they were talking with my landlady. I pulled Martin into a shop until they left, then I went and asked the landlady and she said they were asking about me. She thought I'd done something. She said they'd be coming back and I thought they'd come to take Martin. I stayed indoors till Ali came home and I told him, so we left and stayed with his friends that night, and somebody told us of this place, so we came here. I was sorry we didn't tell you, because you had been so kind to us, and this morning I told Ali to ring you, but not to tell you where I was."

"I persuaded him to because I wanted you to know that as long as your baby is well cared for no one will take him from you."

"Then why did they have to send her, that woman from the Home?"

"Just to visit, because she knew Martin."

"I don't want her to come near me."

"Anyway, now you're here, will you promise to keep in touch with me and not do anything unless you have a chat with me?"

"Yes, I promise."

Christ! I was sounding like a damned schoolmaster.

"Okay, and don't forget. Nobody is trying to take the child away."

She nodded in acceptance.

Outside I asked Miss Martindale:

"Well, what do you think?"

"She certainly had the wind up, didn't she? But she seems all right. I don't think the little boy will come to any harm with her."

Back in the office I made my report, indicating in very positive terms that Mrs Agumsah had been frightened on seeing Miss Richardson at her home; I more than hinted that there was no justification for Miss Richardson's appearance on the scene, as Tower Hill was a long way from Campden Hill where her duties were located. I reported that Mrs Agumsah and her son were well and comfortable and that I would maintain regular contact with them until Mrs Agumsah's application against the Council's Rights and Privileges order was dealt with.

I believe that an inquiry into the case was made at County Hall; about a month later I received a short formal note which stated that recommendations for the removal of children from Council's care would, in future, be sent through the Area Chiefs to County Hall for final decision.

Chapter
Nine

I MIGHT NEVER HAVE heard of the Milnes but for the fact that when Mrs Milne telephoned the Duty Officer was busy with a new applicant, and the two other officers in the building at that time were engaged on interviews. Miss Felden put the call through to me.

Mrs Milne said that she and her husband wished to adopt a small child, preferably a girl, and had been advised to get in touch with our office.

Listening to the clear, precise enunciation, I tried to conjure up a picture to match the voice. Probably between thirty and say, thirty-five. Suburban. Lower middle income bracket. I missed a bit of what she was saying, but gathered that someone acquainted with her had seen an advertisement put out by the Council for foster-parents and adoptive-parents and had passed the telephone number on to her.

I had no idea what the advertisement offered, but assured her that there were children in the Council's care available for adoption, but that it would be best for one of our Welfare Officers to call on her and discuss the matter at a time convenient to herself and her husband. She agreed. Her husband was at work each day but he'd arrange to have some time off to meet the Welfare Officer. Would tomorrow morning at ten o'clock be suitable? I assured her that it would and she gave me her telephone number and address in Wanstead, a London suburb. Not bad guessing, so far. I wrote it down, together with her name and the nature of her inquiry, intending to pass the information on to the Duty Officer, when a little thought entered my head. Why not follow this through myself? Here was an excellent opportunity to test one or two little theories which, so far, were only theories.

Without exception, the dwellings along both sides of Fairview Lane were new bungalows, each set a short distance away from the road, each comfortable and primly squat behind the low, painted wire fence which separated it from its neighbours, and each was fronted by geometrically designed miniature flowerbeds or grass plots, with here and there a shady tree still convalescing from the shock of recent transplantation. In the bright Spring sunshine there was a sugar-candyish look about the smooth, clean street and the bright new houses, as if it had all been created magically, and might just as magically disappear from sight.

I pressed the doorbell at No. 113 and heard the deep three-note chimes, as the door opened and the young woman stood looking at me, her mouth slightly agape in surprise. With an obvious effort she controlled herself to ask:

"Yes?" Sunlight reflected off her rimless spectacles, so I could not see her eyes.

"Mrs Milne?"

"Yes."

"My name is Braithwaite. I'm from the Welfare Department."

Her face paled perceptibly, then flushed.

"Oh, yes, of course. Won't you come in?"

Inside it was cool, new, neat and cosy. She closed the door, then led the way into the sitting-room which looked on to the front garden and the street beyond. A tall, slim man was standing there; he must have risen to greet the visitor, the hand already half-outstretched, the smile ready in welcome, but both these faltered slightly at sight of me. Only slightly. Then we shook hands as I introduced myself.

"When Mrs Milne telephoned I thought it best to come and see you as soon as possible, to brief you on the kind of formalities which surround every application for adoption," I told them.

"Glad you could come," he said, now quite at ease, steering me to a chair. "Would you like a drink or a cup of tea, or something?"

"Tea would be fine."

"Won't be a minute," his wife said, "the kettle's already on," and she left the room, still seeming somewhat in a daze. Without doubt my unheralded appearance had caught them somewhat off balance; a black official was just a little bit outside their experience, but they were adjusting to it very competently.

"You took us by surprise," Mr Milne was saying, "we sort of expected someone else, if you see what I mean."

I saw what he meant and liked his forthright reference to it. I couldn't help smiling, however, at the thought that a black face could still surprise people.

"I understand," I replied. "I'm new to the Welfare Department and most people are a bit surprised when I appear on the scene without any warning, so to speak."

"Silly of me to be surprised, really," he said, "considering my job. I work for the Ministry of Labour and we see all sorts at some time or another."

I let that pass, knowing that he was doing his best to put me at ease. Now his wife returned with a tray from which she placed tea-cups on a low table, then sat beside her husband, still bravely being relaxed and not nervous, in spite of the way the crockery had rattled as she set it out. So, before they could get started on any discussion of children I said: "Years and years ago I knew this district, though this is my first visit to it on foot. During the war I was stationed for a while at Hornchurch aerodrome, and often flew over the surrounding countryside. Gosh, but how it has changed since then! Building projects everywhere, I'm sure there's hardly a single familiar landmark left."

"Oh, you were at Hornchurch?" Mr Milne asked. "My wife was born near there, at Elm Park."

"I knew Elm Park. That was at the far end of the 'drome. Some of us went there on Saturday nights to the local hop."

"The Masonic?" she asked eagerly.

"Sometimes, and there was another place near the railway station."

She nodded, remembering, and mentioned the name.

"I went out to Hornchurch a few weeks ago," I continued, "and could hardly recognize the place. The meadow which once ran alongside the back of the 'drome is now a housing estate. Those lovely oak trees, nearly all cut down. Used to be a stream running along there, the Ingrebourne, the local people called it a river. First time I heard that I laughed till I cried. You know, back home in British Guiana a river is really something, while this little thing in the meadow you could just step across it. But it was fun on a summer's day to watch the clear water rippling over smooth stones at the bottom, or drop the blades of grass on the surface to see them spin in the current."

"Yes, it's all built up now," Mrs Milne said. "Even the aerodrome's changed. I think they use it as a training centre or something like that."

"I noticed that this is a new housing estate."

"Yes, more or less. They began putting houses on this site about four years ago; this section is quite new. When we first came to see the location it was all wasteland. Now, look at it. In five years' time it will be very nice." As she spoke, I was taking a good look at her. She sat near her husband on the settee alongside the window, so that the sunlight on the lacy curtains formed a vague background for the round face around which pale blonde short hair glinted like a halo. Behind her rimless spectacles I got the impression of pale blue eyes, but their expression was effectively veiled by the changing reflections of the glass. Her figure was plump and I had noticed that her movements were quick and energetic.

Her husband was thin; even the waistcoat of his dark grey suit was loose around his skinny frame, and his long neck moved freely away from the stiff white collar and ex-R.A.F. tie. The long, bony face was serious in repose; this may have been due to the unusually bushy eyebrows which twisted outward and upward in a wayward black growth that matched his thick black mop of hair. Now and then he smiled, the thin-lipped wide mouth lifting upward at the corners to disclose a sudden boyishness.

We drank our tea and chatted about the old times, about rationing and buzz-bombs and prefabricated houses and Marshall Aid and the increased bank rate and new housing estates and hospitals and schools and children.

"We lost our little girl three years ago," he said. "Polio. She was just a month over four years. Joyce had a terrible time with the delivery and we were told we cannot have any more. So now we've decided to adopt." His deep, rumbling voice had a very pleasant, friendly quality.

"Why didn't you try one of the adoption societies?" I asked.

"We've talked with various friends and we heard that the adoption societies are mostly concerned with new babies," she replied. "We thought it would be best to take a child who'd got over the nappy stage."

"What type of child did you have in mind?"

"Well, you know how it is," her laughter was a thin, half nervous sound. "We hadn't quite made up our mind about that; sometimes we'd think of one thing and sometimes another. Our little girl was dark, like Phil, but I'd been thinking of a little girl, blonde perhaps. I know Phil would rather have a little boy, but we haven't decided about it. Perhaps when we see them we could sort of make up our mind."

This was quite a speech for her; so far her husband had done most of the talking. Gradually they had become more relaxed and were chatting easily with me; probably the background of shared experiences during the war helped considerably.

"I'm afraid the Department does not operate that way. We try as far as is possible to meet an applicant's preference, but there can be no question of selecting one from a group. If you have a specific preference and we have a child who closely approximates to it, well and good."

"Are there lots of children wanting to be adopted?" he asked.

"Enough," I replied. "Generally we operate rather differently from the regular adoption societies. We encourage applicants first to consider becoming foster-parents. This provides for the closest possible association between parent and child without the final commitment which adoption requires. If the association proves a happy one, then only a few formalities are necessary for the change from fostering to adoption."

"I suppose most of the children have lost their parents?" she asked.

"Yes, in one way or another, though some of them have parents who cannot provide a home. Our main concern is that as many of them as possible might experience what it means to be part of a family, in a real home, with persons they can call 'Mother' and 'Father'. Even a few years of this can be invaluable to a child."

"Are they all English children?"

I thought about that and found it somewhat amusing. "It depends on what you mean by English. With very few exceptions they were born in England and would qualify for the term 'English', although one or both of the parents might have been Irish or Scots or Welsh or West Indian or African or Asian."

"Oh," she said, colouring.

"If we decided to become foster-parents as a first step," Mr Milne said, "do we have any say in the sort of child we take?"

"Oh yes, up to a point."

"I mean can we choose to have a white, English child?" There was a slight note of belligerence in his voice, as if he was daring me to argue with him on that point.

"Why, of course," I replied. "What I meant was that, if that is your preference, we would then tell you if there were any such children available, their ages and sex. When you have decided on the sex and age-range you prefer, we would try to match a child to those requirements and to you."

"Seems fair enough."

"If we take a child do we have full control of her? I mean, can we just bring her up as a member of our family?"

"That's exactly how we hope it would be and the closer it is to that, the more likely the transition to adoption."

We each had another cup of tea, and by this time we were chatting very easily. I had brought some application forms and asked that they complete one of them at their convenience and send it to me.

They showed me over their bungalow, a compact, three-bedroomed building, everything spick and span. From the dining-room, french windows opened on to a lawn of tender new grass bordered by a hedge of dark green privet. Three or four large trees which had escaped the bulldozers and levellers provided sun-dappled shade at the far end of the garden. Plenty of room for a small child, both in and outdoors, I thought.

I received their completed application form two days later, attached it to a short report on my visit to the Milnes and my personal impression of them, and sent it in to the Chief. She would, I knew, send it on to the Area nearest to where the Milnes lived, with a request that the application be followed up by one of their officers.

About two weeks later Mr Milne telephoned me.

"Milne here, Mr Braithwaite; just calling to say I hope you haven't forgotten about us. We were rather hoping to hear from you before now."

I had not forgotten about Mr Milne, but had assumed that the Area Office to which his application had been passed would have contacted him long ago. I tried to reassure him.

"The matter is very much in hand, Mr Milne," I replied. "The delay was due to the processing to which all applications are subjected, but you'll soon be hearing about yours. A Welfare Officer from the Area Office nearest to your home will call around to see you." I made a mental note to check with the office concerned and hurry things up a bit.

"One other thing, Mr Braithwaite; my wife and I have been talking the matter over, and we've decided to have a coloured child."

That stopped me in mid-breath, so to speak, because I had felt sure that he and his wife wanted a child who looked nearly like the little girl they had lost. I was quite unprepared for this.

"Are you there, Mr Braithwaite?"

"Yes, Mr Milne."

"I was saying Joyce and I have decided to have one of the coloured children. A little girl, same age as we put on the form."

"Fine, Mr Milne, we'll see what we can do."

"Will we be hearing from you soon?"

"Within the week, I promise you."

Then I rang the Area Office nearest to Wanstead. I was put in touch with the Welfare Officer to whom the Milne application had been passed.

"Burton here."

"My name is Braithwaite. I think you're dealing with an application from Mr Milne of Wanstead."

"Yes, I have the application." Very much the official.

"I've just had a telephone call from Mr Milne. He and his wife are rather anxious to hear something."

"Sorry about that, but there just hasn't been the time."

"I promised him that someone would call within the week."

"Who did you say you were?"

"Braithwaite." Let him work that one out the best he could!

"Braithwaite, oh yes. Braithwaite . . . Well, I'll get over to see the Milnes as soon as I can."

I had thought of speaking to him of Mr Milne's request for a coloured child but decided against it; they'd discuss it with him when he visited them. My brief talk with Mr Burton left me with a feeling of irritation. No time to follow up an application in more than two weeks—yet we were continually complaining that there were not enough foster-parents. Oh, well, not to panic.

About a week later Mr Milne telephoned again.

"Hello, Mr Braithwaite; one of your colleagues, a Mr Burton, called around to see us."

"Oh good."

"Well, not too good. He did not seem to take too kindly to the idea that we wanted to have a coloured child. He mentioned that there were lots of white children who would benefit more greatly from a comfortable home, and gave the impression that one ran grave risks in fostering black children. I must say that Joyce and I were rather put out by his attitude. At one point she asked him quite pointedly if he disliked the black ones."

"I'm sorry if anything Mr Burton said upset you or your wife," I replied. Although I could not recall having met Mr Burton personally, I could not encourage any criticism of him in this way. "Sometimes we take such a line only to discover how deep and sincere is the interest expressed in fostering a coloured child." I hoped he'd accept that as explanation.

"For whatever reason, we considered his attitude very high-handed and patronizing. He seemed to think that you had suggested the idea to us."

"I might have, if I had thought of it." I laughed, hoping to swing him away from any further discussion about Burton. "Anyway, did you change your mind?"

"Certainly not, neither has Joyce. She can be very stubborn if anyone tries to push her. We insisted that we'd have a coloured child, so he said there were none available in his Area, but he'd check with the other Areas and let us know. I wish you'd look into the matter for us."

"I'll do what I can, Mr Milne."

That afternoon I went to see Mr Burton. A big, thick-set, handsome man, he had once been a truant officer, and had the bearing and gruffness of a policeman. I introduced myself.

"I caught a glimpse of you here a while ago," he said, "but was dashing out and did not meet you. I suppose you've come about the Milne people."

"Yes. They're a bit anxious to hear something soon."

"They've got an idea in their heads that they want to foster a coloured child."

"So?"

"I've met that type of person before. They just want to be different, without stopping to think of the problems involved. Then, after a month or two of having a black child in the house, they shout for us to come and take it away. Especially women who've lost a child and can't have any more. Although they don't know it, they want one that looks as much as possible like the one they lost. I found out that they'd had a little daughter. So I know from experience that a black child just won't do for them."

He spoke with a careful reasonableness which carried me along in agreement, until I said: "But they might be quite sincere. They seem to be mature, balanced people."

"All on the surface; I know from experience. They'd be best advised to have another little white girl. You know," here he smiled, "I can understand you trying to push things for your own people, but we in the Department must always take the long view."

I got the message. He obviously believed that the Milnes had been either influenced or encouraged by me; however I could not be bothered to pursue it.

"Don't you think you should give them the benefit of any doubt and take it for granted that they made their decision after careful, reasoned thinking?" I asked. He was still smiling.

"Somehow it came out that they only began thinking of coloured children *after* you visited them," he continued with heavy emphasis. "If someone from this Area had seen them first the question would never have arisen."

"You mean you never mention coloured children when you meet prospective foster-parents?"

"It's not that we never mention them, but it's most unusual for anyone to ask for a coloured child."

Suddenly I had heard enough from him.

"Look, Mr Burton, as far as I'm concerned, the Milnes have made a direct and reasonable request and it's up to us to do the best we can. If there are no coloured children available in this Area, we can certainly find one in another Area. If you personally do not like the idea of their having a coloured child, some other officer could well handle the case." I had not planned to say this; the words just came out, but without any regret.

He looked at me, his neck reddening above the tight collar of his shirt, but when he spoke his voice remained controlled and the smile struggled to stay on his face.

"Mr Braithwaite, if there's any complaint about the way I'm handling this case, I'm afraid you'll have to take it up with the Area Officer. As I've told Mr and Mrs Milne, we'll do our best to find a child for them, but these things take a little time. I have no prejudice against coloured people, if that's what you're hinting; I merely try to make sure that the right child is placed in the right home. Now, if you'll excuse me, there are several other matters I want to attend to."

There was nothing for me to do but leave him. No point in seeing his Chief, because I had no real complaint to make. I did not see his action as indicating prejudice against coloured people; I didn't think of it that way. But it did seem to me that he was more concerned with placing the white children. It could even be that he saw himself as protecting the black children from persons whose motives were suspect. Too protective. I had no doubt that he believed that his intentions were the best, and I was now rather sorry that I had antagonized him.

Two months later Mr Milne wrote to me.

Dear Mr Braithwaite,

From the very prompt way in which you responded to our first inquiry about adopting a child, my wife and I assumed that your Department was anxiously concerned to find homes or foster-parents for the orphans and other children in your care. It is now more than four months since we made our application to foster a child, yet no action has been taken to help us and nothing has been said to give us hope for action in the near future.

During your visit to us you led us to believe that both white and coloured children in your care needed to be fostered. My wife and I are both practising Christians and decided to give a coloured child the love and comfort which our own little girl would have received if she had lived. We told this to the Welfare Officer who visited us, but we did not find him enthusiastic about the idea, and we wonder if that is the reason our application is still unfulfilled.

A few days ago we decided we would wait no longer, and, on the advice of a friend, we've been in touch with the International Social Service in London. We are determined to have a coloured child and they have promised to help us, so I have written to Mr Burton cancelling our application.

I hope you do not think us either too impatient or precipitate. Our home and hearts are ready for a child and we believe there must be a child somewhere ready for us. I speak for my wife as well as for myself when I say that we were delighted to meet you and hope you will drop in on us whenever you visit Wanstead.

Yours sincerely,
PHILIP MILNE

Chapter
Ten

ONE AFTERNOON, ON MY way upstairs, after lunch, Nancy Drake, that day's Duty Officer, stopped me. "Could you come into the Duty Room for a moment? I'm having a bit of trouble with a family and you might be able to help me."

Although she spoke in her usual quiet tones, the bright red spots on her cheeks showed that she was either scared or angry; angry, I thought, as it would take a great deal to scare Nancy Drake. She was about thirty years old and, no matter what the weather, always dressed in heavy tweed skirts and thick sweaters which did only what she meant them to do, keep her warm. Thick short, curly brown hair framed her pleasant face. She was continually dashing about, always joking, in an excess of robust health and good humour. There was always something sudden about her make-up, something last-minute and rushed, but when she smiled, as she so often did, one had the feeling that problems would get sorted out, somehow. She was not smiling now.

I followed her into the Duty Room. A youngish black man was standing beside her desk, his hat jauntily perched on his head, his stance indicating anger or defiance or both. Near him was seated a young woman, largely pregnant, with a small, frightened-looking boy perched precariously on her knee. They all turned towards the door as I went in, but looked away immediately on seeing me, the little boy clasping his mother tightly and burrowing his head against her. Nancy took her seat behind her desk and I walked over to stand beside her. In retrospect, we must have presented an odd tableau of opposing parties with the desk an insignificant barrier between the two groups. Nancy spoke to them.

"I've asked Mr Braithwaite, one of our Welfare Officers, to come in and help me explain the situation to you." Then to me: "This is Mr James and his wife and small son. Last week we found a place for Mrs James and the boy at Newington Lodge, because the family had been evicted from their room, and the local police had sent them to us, so Mrs James and the boy could be found temporary accommodation. Mrs James is pregnant. Now it seems that Mr James has removed his wife from Newington because she complained she wasn't happy there, and he expects us to find other accommodation for her. I've been trying for nearly an hour to explain to him that we have no other available accommodation, but he doesn't seem inclined to believe me."

While she had been speaking I was closely observing Mr James. About thirty-five years of age, tidy of dress, but in need of a shave. Slim, even skinny, his face looked grim under the wide-brimmed black felt hat. A hand-made cigarette drooped from his mouth, and his eyes were squinted nearly shut against the smoke. There was an empty chair beside his wife, but he remained standing.

"If you'd sit down, Mr James, we might be able to chat more comfortably about this," I said. He glared at me without replying for a while, his mouth twisted in a mocking smile.

"I'm not leaving my wife with those people, in that place." The cigarette bobbed up and down as he spoke.

"If you'd sit down it would be easier to discuss the matter," I repeated.

"Sit down, Leopold," his wife said, touching the chair beside her. He turned to look at her, then again at me; I sat in the chair beside Miss Drake, so he must have felt rather out of place standing alone. Finally, resentfully, he sat down.

"You've forgotten one little thing, Mr James. There are ladies present," I said, looking pointedly at his head. With a smooth, angry motion, he swept his hat off his head and dropped it on the floor beside his chair.

"And now, Mr James, if you please, I'd like to hear your side of the matter."

He bent his head, puffing his cigarette and glaring at me sideways. He seemed in no hurry to reply, so I let him take his time. Eventually he said: "The police sent me here last week after the landlord put us out, and they (he meant our Department) sent my wife and son to that Lodge place. I had to go and sleep on the floor at my friend's place. Every time I go to see my wife she's crying because the women there don't talk to her. So I take her away this morning. I don't want my wife to stay in no place where the people don't talk to you. They shouldn't send her to a place where the white women won't talk to her."

"Why were you turned out of your room, Mr James?"

"I haven't been working and the landlord won't wait for his rent. I've been sick for three months now."

Mr James may easily have been telling the truth, but he looked reasonably fit to me.

"But it was mostly because my wife is expecting again; he said he won't have any more children in the house so we'd have to leave. What kind of law is it that lets them put a pregnant woman on the streets?"

"We can't intervene between you and the law, Mr James. I understand that the police sent you to us after you were evicted."

"Yes."

"And Miss Drake made arrangements for your wife and son to be accommodated at Newington Lodge while you looked around for alternative accommodation?"

"Yeah, but they shouldn't . . . "

"How do you support yourself and wife, Mr James?"

"What?"

"I'd like to know how you've been supporting your wife and son and yourself."

"While I'm not working I get National Assistance." His eyes hated me as he said it. "But why are you asking me all that? The white woman didn't ask me all that."

"I'm not doing it to pry into your affairs, Mr James, but merely to help you to understand the situation. Let's put it this way. You are unemployed and cannot at the moment properly support your wife and child, not to mention the other child on the way. Because of those and probably other reasons, your wife and son were in Newington Lodge. Now you've removed them from there. What do you plan to do with them now, Mr James?"

He jumped up angrily, and as an added gesture, reached under his chair for his hat and stuck it atop his head, then pointed a long, bony arm at me until the index finger with its blackened nail was only a few inches from my face. I think I was getting under his skin, way down deep.

"Would you let a woman of yours stay in a place like that where none of them white bitches would even talk to her?" He was hopping mad, and using it to swing the matter to his favour.

"It so happens that no woman of mine is involved in this matter, Mr James, so that question is quite irrelevant. I do hope you realize that by removing them you have taken the matter completely out of our hands. Now what do you plan to do with them?"

"Sit down, Leopold," his wife admonished, quietly.

Leopold, indeed. In that small room the name had overtones which did not quite fit the angry, bullying fellow. He sat down sulkily, making it seem that he only did so to please his wife; this time the hat remained on his head.

"What do you want us to do, Mr . . . ?" Her voice was barely audible, but there was dignity in every line of her face; the difficulties and abuses which had brought her to this state had not robbed her of that.

"What has it been like for you at the Lodge?" I asked.

"I have a little room, a cubicle they call it or something like that, and I've been staying in it most of the time, mostly because of Edgar." She favoured the boy with a smile, but he was still tightly clinging to her, like a tiny koala bear to its mother. "He's very shy and wouldn't leave me to play with the other children."

"Have you had any difficulty with the other women?"

"Well, they didn't say anything, so I go down to meals and afterwards go back to my room."

"Mrs James, all the women at Newington Lodge are in very much the same situation as yourself. None of them likes to be there, but they try to make the best of it until their husbands can find them something better. I've been into the Lodge and talked with some of them. Perhaps they're just as shy as you are, but I have an idea they try to help each other. You may be quite right when you say they won't talk to you, but we don't know for sure, do we? Probably if you showed yourself willing to be friendly it might help things along, don't you think?"

"I suppose so," she whispered. Her voice was so quiet and her whole manner so pathetic, I was somewhat ashamed of myself for bullying her husband, but I felt it was the only way to deal with him in this instance. He had very likely been giving Nancy Drake a tough time earlier on.

"And now, Mr James?"

"I got no place to take them," he said. "I brought them here because I thought if she didn't like it there you'd send her somewhere else."

"As Miss Drake has already explained, we have no other available accommodation."

"Then I suppose they'll have to go back there. But I don't like the idea."

"Then the best thing you can do is find a job and get them out of there . . . " He glared at me, as I added, " . . . if you really want to."

"I don't know if the room is still available," Nancy interposed. "There are so many people wanting rooms that the Superintendent can't keep them empty. I'd better telephone and see." She picked up the phone and after a short delay managed to reach the Superintendent at Newington Lodge. Then followed a long argument, with Nancy using all her powers of persuasion on that gentleman, who, from what I could hear of the one-sided conversation, was not anxious to welcome Mrs James again, entirely because of the unfavourable impression her husband had created. However, Nancy won through. I was rather pleased that Mr James had overheard her efforts on his wife's behalf, because that more than anything else finally convinced him of the seriousness of his position. When the arrangements were concluded, he had the final word.

"I'll go to the Labour Exchange and see about a job tomorrow. I don't want my wife to stay in that place a day longer than I can help. It's like a bloody prison. A man can't visit with his wife after ten o'clock at night. Bloody prison."

Nancy ushered them out and came back wiping imaginary sweat from her forehead with a crooked forefinger.

"Whew! What a creep! Until you came in he had me sort of backed against the wall and I couldn't do a thing with him. Thanks, chum."

"Any time."

"I must try that sometimes if I can work up enough guts. Gosh, you were tough with him—even I was feeling sorry for him."

"Maybe now he's sufficiently mad at me to really get a job and do something for his wife, but I doubt it. He's the kind who'd be very happy to sit on his behind and let the State look after him and any others he happens to father. I've met that type before."

I was a lousy prophet. Two weeks later Mr James took his wife and son out of Newington Lodge; he'd got a job as a railway porter and found a room for them in Clapham. A small room, but they were together. Perhaps I had made him angry enough to do it, or perhaps he had planned to do it before my intervention. I'll never know.

Wednesday morning I had a call from Matron. She sounded a bit anxious and I agreed to call on her that afternoon.

"Trouble?" I asked as we shook hands.

"Not much, but enough."

"Roddy?"

"Yes. Mr Tamerlane brought him back here early Monday morning and he was just like a puppy with three tails wagging all at once. He came in here and told me all about what he had done over the weekend. It was 'Mummy' and 'Dad' and 'Junie' and 'Jackie', as natural as you please, as if he had always been part of the family. I heard that Uncle Ricky and Auntie Olga had been to tea, among other things. Well, he got changed into his house-clothes and went in to join the others in the play room. Naturally he was eager to tell them all about it, but little Miss Fixit had to interfere."

"Who?"

"Natalie Mays."

"The little blonde fireball?"

"Yes."

"What did she do?" Listening to Matron I quickly got the clear, disturbing picture of the incident. Roddy, all excitement, had rushed up to the others with:

"My daddy brought me back in his car."

"You haven't got a daddy." That was Natalie.

"I have too, got a daddy. I went with daddy and mummy and Junie and Jackie, and we had tea and climbed a big tree with a swing. And Uncle Ricky had tea with us and Auntie Olga. And we had a picnic in Epping Forest." Half-breathless, with the dark brown eyes aglow.

"What's Epping Forest?" asked Natalie, always the spokesman and moving spirit among the small fry.

"It's lots of trees and grass with lots of people sitting down, and cars. And I had a game with Junie and Jackie. And daddy bought us iced lollies."

"He's only a make-believe daddy," Natalie again. "You haven't a real daddy like me."

"I have too, Uncle Ricky says so."

"Your Uncle Ricky is black."

"He's not a make-believe daddy."

"He is too, he is, he is." And she kept repeating it like a terrible persistent refrain.

It proved too much for Roddy and he had run to Miss Schroeder, the sudden tears streaking his face, and flung himself into her arms, crying, "He isn't a make-believe daddy, is he, Miss Ann, is he, is he?"

Miss Schroeder had done her best to comfort him and had taken him with her when she went shopping later that morning.

"How is he now?" I asked.

"None the worse for it, but he's not easily moved to tears, so Natalie's words must have cut deep."

I went into the playroom where, as usual, they were engaged with their several games. Roddy was delighted to see me, and I gave him the parcel of sweets. He sat on the floor and opened it. There was an assortment of hard sweets which I thought would please him. He took some in each hand, gave one to me then went to each of his little friends in turn, beginning with Natalie. I had the idea that she was a kind of Queen Bee among them.

Soon after, one pink jaw distended with toffee, she came over to me and stood, feet apart, her chubby hands cuddling a one-legged doll to her chest, her pretty face tilted upwards.

"Are you Roddy's Uncle Ricky?"

"Yes."

"Can you be my Uncle Ricky too?"

"I suppose I could."

"And Paula's and Mervin's?"

"Yes, and Paula's and Mervin's."

"But you're black."

"Wouldn't you like to have a black Uncle Ricky?"

"My daddy says I can't have a black uncle, only Roddy can have a black uncle."

I let that go. The absent Mr Mays was having a hand in the game, like dummy hand in bridge.

"Will Roddy's daddy take him away?"

"Perhaps."

"My daddy will take me away very soon."

"That will be nice."

"Is Roddy's daddy a make-believe daddy?"

"Daddies are never 'make-believe'. Make-believe people are in fairy books."

Roddy was watching carefully and listening hard although he pretended to be busy re-making the parcel of sweets.

"My dolly has lost her leg. Paula calls her dolly 'Mary Jane.'" And with that she turned away to resume the game from which the whim had diverted her. I left them and went to Matron's office.

"Children can be the cruellest people without intending any harm," she said, "that's why I always say that truth is a strange concept. Well, he'll have to learn to take the rough with the smooth."

Now that Roddy's case had progressed so far I was impatient to have it settled; probably I was afraid that because it had moved so smoothly, it was all a prelude to some big disappointment. In the days that followed it required a great deal of effort to keep me from pestering the Chief for news of progress with Middlesex, but the increasing load of cases kept me busy enough to prevent preoccupation with it. In spite of my best intentions I could not consider my attitude to that or most of the other cases truly objective. Upon self-examination I realized that I was consistently breaking what might be called a cardinal rule for Welfare Officers, I was 'caring' about my cases, becoming too involved with them. One day I discussed this with Jim Baxter.

"I started in much the same way," he said, "but I've managed to cure myself, at least, up to a point."

"How did you do that?"

"By coming to a sort of arrangement with myself. As I begin each new case I tell myself that I dislike the people concerned, but that I've got a job to do in helping them. Then it's easy to help them without becoming emotionally involved."

"Odd," I said. "I always thought that dislike is as emotional as like."

"Look, I'm only telling you how I approach the work; you can make up your own mind and decide on your own attitude to it. But remember, you've got to play the game according to the rules, and let's make no mistake about it, chum, this is a kind of game."

"Heads I win, tails you lose?"

"What's that supposed to mean?"

"If we win, somebody loses, and as I see it, the poor blighters who come to us for help can't win, if we are to accept your definition of the game."

"The thing is not to care."

"But I thought the prime motive behind our work was the fact that we cared, or were supposed to?"

"Don't preach at me," Baxter said, "of course one cares, but only in general terms. As soon as the caring becomes particular you're asking for trouble. Let me put it this way. I care for my wife and little girl emotionally, because my life is closely involved with them;

I care for these others in a kind of scientific way, because I would like to see each case finally and happily resolved. But I don't let it get to me, inside me I mean. At the beginning of each case I remind myself that I don't know any of the people concerned; when the case is ended I want to be able to forget it quickly, as if it never happened, so I can have my mind free to deal with the next problem."

"And it works?"

"You're damned right it works," he laughed.

Perhaps he was right. Perhaps if I remained in the Department as long as he had, I too would discover the trick of arresting my interest just short of caring, or involvement. Perhaps. The trouble was I kept forgetting to limit myself. This fellow Baxter was so sure that he was right. That idea of disliking the people concerned in each new case. I didn't really believe him. One could not create a dislike of people one had never seen, or could one? I had already found myself disliking some people, but only after meeting them. And I found it difficult to be pleasant with people I disliked. Mrs Larkin for instance.

I was alone in the office the Saturday morning when the call came in from the police. A young mother of three small children had had a heart attack and died suddenly. The grief-stricken young husband was in a state of shock and quite unable to do much for the children, two small boys of four and two and a half years, and a new baby; the police had been called by neighbours and their opinion was that we should take the children into the Council's care until the father recovered sufficiently to be able to make plans for them.

Remembering previous experiences, I rang through to County Hall and made arrangements for the children to be received—the boys at a children's home and the baby girl at a residential nursery—then I set out to find the address the police sergeant had given me.

Mr Pridie, the bereaved husband, occupied a small first-floor flat in one of the new London County Council housing projects not far from New Cross railway terminal. I knocked on his door several times without receiving any reply and was thinking of checking with the police station when the door of the apartment next to his was opened by a middle-aged woman. At first she seemed surprised to see me, then her face settled into a stiff, unpleasant mask out of which her pale blue eyes regarded me with cold hostility.

"Good morning, I'm trying to locate Mr Pridie."

She regarded me for several lengthy moments without replying, then called over her shoulder.

"Joe," in a sharply penetrating voice. I wondered whether I had knocked on the wrong door by mistake, and quickly looked down at the piece of paper I still held in my hand. No mistake, the address was 47b Ravensmead House, and I had knocked at 47b. The woman had come out of No. 48. Someone replied gruffly behind her and presently she moved aside to allow a tall, heavy-set man to stand beside her. They made an oddly interesting pair. He wore shapeless grey flannel trousers, and a thin, sleeveless summer vest under which his thick, hairy torso bulged unattractively. His heavy face was a web of bluish capillaries, and the thick red nose and the dark pendulous pouches under his eyes added a bizarre touch of dissipation. His eyes, like the woman's, were pale, watery blue, but here the resemblance ended. She was clean without achieving neatness, and there was no warmth in any of her features; she had the look of having been milked deep of every last vestige of humour.

"What's up?" he asked, and I nearly burst out laughing from a mixture of relief and shock. The voice which came out of him was surprisingly high-pitched, as if it had been nestling somewhere high in his chest, ready to slip out at the first chance of release.

"He's asking for Pridie." Now she folded her arms across the flat chest. I remember thinking to myself, 'You ought to exchange clothes, you two, he'd fill that jumper a hell of a lot better.'

"What does he want with him?" Although I was standing there close to him, he addressed his question to her.

She looked at me, evidently expecting me to provide the answer, the dislike providing the only thing which came close to animation in her eyes. I suddenly decided to keep my mouth shut and see how far they would carry their ridiculous attitude. After a few minutes of silence she said:

"What do you want with him?"

"I'd like to talk with him. Is he in?"

"What about?"

"It's a private matter."

"Is he one of them you've been telling me about, who've been coming here to the Pridies?" he asked her. I wondered why he would not ask me.

"I don't know; I don't think I've seen this one before." As she spoke, her eyes travelled slowly over me, missing nothing.

"You a friend of his?"

"No. I am a Welfare Officer. I am here about his children."

They exchanged glances. He looked sharply at me, but there was no change in her cold attention.

"Who sent you?"

I was suddenly angry. Who the hell did she think she was putting me through this questionnaire? Now it was my turn.

"Why? Are you related to him?" That seemed to take some of the wind out of her sails.

"Do you know what happened?" he asked me.

"The police reported that his wife died suddenly this morning, so I am here to find out what's happening about the children." This time I made my voice as authoritative as possible.

"The children are here, with us," he offered, before she could reply; she turned to glare at him as if annoyed that he should have given me the information.

"And Mr Pridie?"

"He's out, but he said he was coming back soon."

"May I see the children?"

This time she beat him to it, her attitude pointedly unfriendly. "No. We can't let anyone see them without their father's permission."

"So what difference does it make?" her husband interposed. "Let him see them if he wants to."

"Not in my house. No nigger's coming into my house." The viciousness of the words shocked me, although I was aware from the moment of meeting her that she either disliked me on sight or was antipathetic to people of my skin colour. But her words seemed so unnecessary and unreasonable that a hot reply jumped into my mouth and it was only with very great difficulty that I swallowed it.

"Well, for Christ's sake!" her husband exclaimed. "What the hell's got into you? If the authorities sent him to see the kids what do you have to take on like that for?"

"This is my house and I'm not letting any nigger come inside it," she replied calmly, evidently pleased with herself and enjoying the thought that she was causing me embarrassment.

Just then footsteps could be heard ascending the stairs from the ground floor, and soon a neatly dressed, dark-skinned young man appeared and walked around us to 47b, a bunch of keys jangling in his hand. He had barely glanced at us.

"There's Pridie," the man said.

What's in a name? Come to think of it, not much. Yet so often one is predisposed to create a person to suit a name newly heard. Until this moment it had never occurred to me that Mr Pridie was anything but European and English. More than that. It had not occurred to me that Mr Pridie would be anything but white-skinned. In my conversation with the police sergeant nothing had been said to lead me to believe otherwise. But why should I be surprised? Surely this was the very thing I had long been agitating for, yet here it was and my first reaction was surprise. God, without realizing it, I was being conditioned into the very same attitude which I claimed I disliked and which I publicly opposed at every opportunity. I suppose I must have stood there gaping stupidly, because the man spoke again.

"Thought you said you wanted Pridie."

By this time the young man had gone into the room and closed the door. I knocked. He opened the door and then I saw his face. He looked stunned or drugged, and shook his head quickly as if trying desperately to focus his attention.

"Mr Pridie?"

"Yes, I'm Pridie."

"I'm a Welfare Officer from . . . "

"Come in, come in," he interrupted, pushing the door wide open and standing aside to let me in. I walked into a small, but comfortable sitting-room, somewhat disarranged, with quite a scattering of children's toys. He casually brushed some of these from a sofa on to the floor, and invited me to sit down.

"Like a drink?" he asked.

"No, thanks, too early in the day for me."

"You won't mind if I have one?" He went through a door

which probably connected with the kitchen, and returned soon afterwards with a glass. I guessed that it contained whisky.

"What were those two telling you?" he asked abruptly.

"Not much. I had just arrived and was inquiring about you. The woman seemed less than friendly."

"That bitch, I can't figure her out. I guess she hates my guts, yet she was the first to appear when Vi fell down. She's got the children over there."

"Yes, so her husband told me."

"She give you a hard time?"

"She tried to, but I've met the type before."

"Boy, she really hates anything black. Because of her son, I guess. They sent him up for cutting a black fellow at a club in Stepney."

"I see."

"Like hell, you see. Boy, if there's one thing that old bag knows how to do it's hate. Funny. She used to meet Vi and me on the stairs or in the street and she'd look straight at us and say, 'Morning, Mrs Pridie,' then pass on just as if I was invisible or something. I just can't figure her. And she's always buying things for the kids, sweets and things, but she's never so much as said a word to me all the time I've lived here."

He got up to open a window, then resumed his seat. Then he placed the glass on the floor beside him, clutched his head in his hands and began to sob; dry tearing sobs that seemed to rend the very foundations of his being. I could think of nothing to say to him, nothing adequate, that is.

After a while he got up and went into an adjoining room, but soon returned with a large blue towel slung around his neck.

"Sorry about that," he said, "but I can't get used to Vi not being here. It's all been so blasted sudden. Yesterday she was sitting right there, fussing with the kids, right there." He pointed at the sofa.

"You have my sincere sympathy, Mr Pridie."

"Thank you. It was her heart, you know. While she was having Marie, our last baby, the doctor warned her, and she's been taking it easy. She wasn't sick, or anything. It was about five o'clock this morning. I didn't even know she had got out of bed. Then I heard this noise in the kitchen, you know, things breaking. I rushed in and there she was, all crumpled up on the floor.

"Suppose she had got up to fix a bottle for the baby, or something. I don't even know if she called for me or anything. I picked her up and put her in our bed and covered her up, you know, to keep her warm. I thought she had fainted or something. And I went downstairs to telephone for the doctor. But she was dead.

"The doctor came and he must have called the ambulance and the police. Then Mrs Larkin came and said she'd look after the kids."

"The police telephoned us," I told him, "I didn't know what the situation was here, so I've made arrangements for the children to be looked after at one of the L.C.C. Homes for the time being. That is, unless you have other plans. They can stay there for a week or two to be out of the way while you sort things out."

"Okay. You work for the L.C.C?"

"Yes, I'm a Welfare Officer."

"Oh, yes. You told me. Where are you from?"

"British Guiana."

"My dad was West Indian. I was born here in London. Forest Hill. Vi's English."

"Can I see the children?"

"Let's go next door and ask her."

Once again I was outside No. 48. Mr Pridie knocked on the door and it was quickly opened, as if someone was half-expecting us.

"This is the Welfare Officer," Mr Pridie explained. "He'd like to see the children."

The woman he had called Mrs Larkin was as uncompromising as ever.

"What does he want with them?"

Her whole attitude was objectionable, deliberately so. I spoke up.

"I've arranged for them to be cared for at one of the L.C.C.'s Children's Homes until Mr Pridie can make alternative plans for them."

"Joe!" She called behind her, "bring the boys here." Then to Mr Pridie, "Why do you want to send the nippers away?"

"Look, I didn't send for him. The doctor or police or somebody sent him here to see about the kids," he retorted.

There was movement behind her, and she shifted slightly in the doorway, just enough to allow two small boys to push past. As I looked down at them, I suddenly thought of Miss Coney. How would she label these? They were both lovely, chubby children; I have seen many an indigenous Briton much darker of skin. These two boys would pass unnoticed in any group of English children; their thick curling brown hair might have suggested, to the purist, southern Italian ancestry, while the thin delicate noses reminded me very much of a French fighter pilot I once knew. I wondered about their mother. No doubt she had been beautiful, to produce such fine specimens. They went to Mr Pridie and hugged his legs, while he mussed their heads, absently. Now, gently, but firmly, Mrs Larkin drew the children back and pushed them back indoors behind her, then folded her arms across her chest and faced us defiantly.

"Well, now you've seen them."

I was at a loss for words; I had no idea how to deal with this situation and, in his present state, Mr Pridie was no better able to cope with it.

"I've explained to Mr Pridie that I've reserved places for them . . . " I began, but she cut me off in mid-sentence.

"Then you can go right ahead and un-reserve whatever it is you've done. I'm sure Mrs Pridie wouldn't want her children put into no Home. They can stay right where they are. If you want them out of here you can go along and fetch the police."

"Mr Pridie did not tell me you had agreed to take care of them," I said.

"Somebody has to," she replied. "When his wife is put away and he can look after them himself he can let me know." And with that she stepped backward into her flat and closed the door on us.

Mr Pridie looked at me resignedly, and led the way back to his room.

"One of these days I'm gonna tell that old battleaxe exactly where she gets off," he said.

'Like hell you will,' I thought. After that little set-to of a few moments ago, I just could not see him telling her anything, either off or on.

"Well, what will you do now?" he asked.

"Nothing. All we're concerned to know is that the children are being well looked after. I am of the opinion that they will come to no harm with Mrs Larkin, so there's nothing for me to do. Besides, you're here, on the spot, to see them at any time. If, later on you definitely decide to place them in a Home, we can take the matter up again, but meanwhile I would suggest that we leave them where they are."

"Christ, she's a funny one. I really believe she loves those kids. Where can I reach you?"

I gave him one of my cards.

"Hell, we work for the same firm," he exclaimed, smiling. "I'm at County Hall, Architects' Division. Look, I've got to do all kinds of running around today. Can I drop you off some place?"

His car was parked downstairs, so I rode with him to New Cross Station. He was silent all the way, but his face betrayed nothing of the deep grief he felt. A dark skin has all kinds of advantages.

Chapter
Eleven

ANOTHER MONDAY MORNING AND another urgent message from Matron. Roddy was in bed with a cold and could I come over as soon as was conveniently possible? What now, I wondered.

During the morning, the Chief telephoned me. There had been a high-level meeting between the Middlesex people and our Directorate at County Hall; she was expecting to have news of their decision some time during the day and would keep me informed. I told her that I would be in the office all morning and planned to visit Franmere in the afternoon; she could probably contact me there between two and four o'clock if the news arrived during that time.

"We had a bit of a 'do' last Saturday," Matron said, by way of greeting. "Roddy is in bed with a cold. Nothing serious, but I'm rather concerned."

"Something happened?"

"Sort of. Roddy was expecting Mr Tamerlane to call Saturday afternoon as promised, and was all dressed and waiting. Just before two o'clock Mr Tamerlane telephoned. He was having trouble with his car and would be late arriving. I told Roddy that his daddy would be late, but that he would come, and left him here by the front door to look out for his arrival. Usually he is a very obedient child and so I did not worry about him, there were lots of other things claiming my attention.

"About four o'clock it began to rain; about half an hour later one of the attendants came into my office and asked me if Mr Tamerlane had called for Roddy as he was nowhere around. I knew that Mr Tamerlane would not have taken him away without informing me or another member of staff, so I told her to look around for Roddy. She found him at the main gate down the drive, soaking wet in the rain, looking hopefully up the road and crying his eyes out. You know, I think he's been brooding over Natalie's remarks.

"However we gave him a hot bath and put him to bed. Mr Tamerlane arrived soon after five o'clock, but he agreed with me that it would be unwise to take him out then. He went up and sat awhile with him and yesterday the whole family, dog and all, came to visit him. He's okay so far, but I think the sooner we place him with a family the better."

"Do you think I've been too precipitate in having him visit the Tamerlanes before the difficulties with Middlesex were cleared up?"

"No, I don't think it matters. For a sensitive child like him, seeing other children with fathers, mothers or other visitors must have affected him, when no one ever called to see him, week after week. He needed someone to love as much as he needed to be loved, and I'm sure the children here realize that he staff are somewhat different from mothers and aunties."

"Should we have a word with the Tamerlanes to restrict their visiting until we know what Middlesex will do?"

"That would not improve the situation with Roddy; he has already accepted them unreservedly. Right now it's not a matter of whether he goes to stay with them, but whether he sees them regularly. Especially Mr Tamerlane, so that he can prove to the other children that he has a daddy, just like anybody else."

I stayed there talking with Matron until four o'clock, apart from a short visit upstairs with Roddy. Although I enjoyed talking with her, I was, most of the time, listening in the hope of receiving a call from my Chief. I said nothing of this to Matron; no more false leads for me.

There was no call for me. I had one or two visits to make before going home, so I'd just have to wait until tomorrow for any news of the meeting.

On my way home that evening my mind often turned to Mr Pridie and his neighbours, the Larkins. Especially Mrs Larkin. Mr Pridie had mentioned that her son was in prison for attacking a West Indian with a knife. Did her anti-black attitude spring from her son's difficulties? Or was she always like that? At this very moment she was probably preparing the Pridie children for bed, or bathing them, or feeding them, or maybe telling them bedtime stories. Smiling at them. Did she smile? Probably she reserved her venom and spite for grown-ups and allowed only the harmless and helpless within the inner sanctum of her warmth and love. Somehow her deliberate rudeness had not really upset me, probably because she was trying too hard, I don't know. What would have been the outcome if one of my white colleagues had called on Mr Pridie? The same, very likely, except that Mrs Larkin might have been less vicious. I wondered if, caring for the children day by day, she felt them tugging at her long-dormant maternal instincts. Could she love them and completely ignore their paternal origin? How about

Roddy's mother? Did she really succeed in forgetting that she had borne a son? Did she really not care? Once upon a time I had read somewhere that it was easy to be a parent, but tough being a mother. Or was it the other way round? What was Miss Williams, mother or parent? If tomorrow I saw her and told her that the boy was ill and calling for her, would there be a change of attitude? Probably not. After all, she did not know him, could certainly not remember him, so he was merely a vague and rather painful experience.

In all this, my contact with the Pridies and Larkins, the Benthams and Tamerlanes and all the others, did I achieve any more or less because of my black skin? I thought not. I think I am naturally of a friendly disposition. That helped, I am sure; but there was nothing unusual or special about that. Most of my colleagues were equally friendly disposed. My black skin did not adversely affect my relationship with the Tamerlanes or Olga or my colleagues, and I don't suppose it was of any special advantage in dealing with Mr James.

So, perhaps, there was something else, and whatever it was, it could as well be employed by any other Welfare Officer. I'd have to prove it, by taking on cases which were not specifically concerned with black persons. The Pridie case was purely accidental. Funny about Pridie. He mentioned that his father had been a West Indian, but said nothing about his mother. He was obviously of mixed parentage, so he left me to assume that his mother was white. Born in a community where colour was an important factor, he had long ago been pressured into alignment, so, without actually saying so, he was obliquely identifying himself with West Indians, to avail himself of whatever spiritual comfort such an alignment brought. Perhaps he never said, "My mother's English." To an English person such a remark would evoke nothing but distaste, at least. But he'd mentioned that his wife was English. That was something else, and it explained his children, who looked so unlike him. What a hell of a situation for human beings to be in; always looking around, like chameleons, for protective cover. How would his sons, in turn, feel about their father, especially now that there was no mother with whom they could identify their 'whiteness'? Would they, by example, be infected by Mrs Larkin's irrational attitude . . . ?

Next morning I heard the news. Middlesex had agreed to our proposal to pay the Tamerlanes over and above the normal rates for foster-parents. But they insisted that the case should not be used as a precedent, and indicated that they could not guarantee other similar requests would be favourably considered. I was delighted. As for the probability of similar situations arising in the future, I, too, would not guarantee that, if the circumstances warranted, I would not follow the same procedure. My business was to find foster-parents, not to worry about matters of principle or precedent; but I kept that thought to myself.

"However,"—the Chief's level voice and controlled features gave no hint of the satisfaction which I was sure she felt—"we shall still proceed cautiously with the case. The boy will continue to visit the Tamerlanes, and either I or Miss Whitney will arrange to drop in on them, to get what you might call an objective view of things. Meanwhile, I wouldn't say much to them about Middlesex, if I were you. By all means hint as broadly as possible that it seems there will be no further objection, and leave it there. I need hardly tell you it will be a relief to see this case finally closed."

I wondered how she did it. With that kind of personal discipline she should be taking on bigger things, but . . .

Now that the uncertainties were at an end I felt somewhat at a loss, but was kept too busy to worry about that. I wrote a short note to the Matron at Franmere telling her of the developments; from now on it was merely a matter of deciding on the time for the change over.

During the month that followed I did not see Roddy, but kept in touch with Matron who informed me that he was spending each weekend with the Tamerlanes and thoroughly enjoying himself. Miss Whitney had 'dropped in' on one such occasion and had made a very favourable report, so everything was doing very nicely, thank you.

I had my hands full with some of the so-called 'black' cases and each one merely served to convince me that there was nothing 'special' about them. I talked with Miss Wren about this but made no headway against her firm opinions on that matter. She mentioned certain cases which had been successfully resolved after they were transferred to me and, I feel sure, she actually believed that the key to that success was my understanding of 'my people'. Perhaps she was right, but for the wrong reasons. 'My people' were not only the black ones; they were all the unfortunates temporarily down on their luck, needing a helping hand; and they were the Benthams and Tamerlanes, the Rosenbergs, the taxi driver, all those who did not limit their love and kindliness by the unprobable barriers of colour or caste, or creed. And if I had any doubt, the memory of the taxi driver washing and dressing the twins with all the skilful tenderness of a loving parent was enough to reassure me. Oh, well, the important thing was to get the cases cleared up, no matter whose 'people' they were.

I fell into the habit of reviewing each case with which I dealt, with as much care as possible, not only for the purpose of keeping useful records, but in order to evaluate my own usefulness. It is true to say that my approach to the cases was somewhat different from that employed by others, but essentially the same in attitude. Time and time again it was clear that anyone else could have been as effective, probably more so. Then there was the offshoot from cases dealt with; the word went around and occasionally, black applicants would specifically request that I see them. On these occasions I saw the applicant, but at the earliest opportunity emphasized that I was not there to provide any special service which any of my colleagues could not as efficiently provide, and, whenever possible, I would turn the applicant over to the Duty Officer or someone else . . .

There was a birthday party at Franmere for Roddy. Matron rang me the day before and invited me to attend. It would be held on the Friday, because he would be collected as usual on the Saturday by the Tamerlanes; only this time his weekend visit would be extended until, without his noticing it, he had become settled in. This process had been discussed and decided upon between Matron and the Tamerlanes. The birthday party was not being laid on as a special event; just the normal tea-time at the Home, but with a birthday cake, candles, and a few gifts. The Tamerlanes were not invited, he'd be seeing enough of them in the normal course of events, but his Auntie Olga had been invited. Matron had rung her and she'd agreed to be present.

I'm never much good at children's parties, I cannot throw myself into the general mêlée of juvenile games, yet I enjoyed being part of it, moving around the edge of it, so to speak. Olga was different, she seemed to be in her element, and knew all those variations on the old ring games. She was dressed for the occasion in black sweater, fine-pleated grey wool skirt and soft, low-heeled 'loafer' shoes. She evidently loved Roddy and seized every opportunity to hug him without becoming too sloppy. None of this escaped Matron. I was having a quiet cigarette from a vantage point near a window, and she came up to me.

"She'll miss him." I looked over to where Olga was kneeling on the floor, chanting as lustily as the others, her face flushed, eyes shining and hair slightly in disarray.

"Not really. She can always see him at the Tamerlanes."

"You think so?"

"Of course, Matron. Why not?"

She merely smiled at me and walked away.

Monday morning there was a letter from Mrs Bentham. I think I read it through several times before the message really sank in. It ran:

Dear Mr Braithwaite,

I don't really know how to begin to say what I want to tell you, because I haven't yet got over the surprise of it, and maybe you won't be able to believe it yourself. Anyway, here it is. Something that should happen has not been happening for nearly three months, and I thought that perhaps it was the *change*. I thought it was a bit soon for me, but I didn't worry too much; after all, it wouldn't make much difference to me one way or another, I thought. Well, the other day I felt quite sick and went around to see my doctor. He's the doctor I've signed up with since moving down here, and he's very nice. Jewish, I think. Well, he examined me, and what do you think? I'm *pregnant!* Me. After all these years. I just couldn't believe it. Can you? The doctor said that it sometimes happens this way. Years of trying and nothing happening, then suddenly it happens. The doctor said I've got nothing to worry about because I'm very fit.

I don't really know how I feel about it, besides being very glad. Funny, I haven't told Jim yet. I don't know how to tell him. I feel sort of embarrassed, like a little girl. I told the doctor about the other baby, you know, the little girl, and he said that maybe that's why it's happened. He said that sometimes it's like that, that looking after her had an effect on me. Psychological, he called it. I looked it up in the dictionary. Don't laugh. The funny thing is that since then I've been looking at the baby, you know, looking to see if I can see anything of Jim in her. You see, perhaps after all, she is his baby. Isn't life strange. Gosh, it's going to be funny with two babies, this one so fair and the other is sure to be black. What will people say? Oh, well, not to worry. Gosh, I wonder how Jim will take it? Oh dear, remember what I said to you that first time you came to see us? Gosh, I feel so silly. What's he going to say? I'm so pleased I could cry.

Do come to see us soon. It's really nice out here, and I'm sure you'll like it. I'll tell Jim when he comes in from work tonight. Do you think he'll be pleased? What about the little boy you spoke of? Hope everything is going fine for him. If you can come soon, send us a card.

Yours very truly,
Marva Bentham

So Mr James Bentham had had the last laugh after all. Mr Man had done his job most manfully. Perhaps, once started, there'd be no stopping him.

About four months later I was in the vicinity where the Tamerlanes lived, and called in. It was about half past three in the afternoon and Ella answered the door, all dressed to go out, but she made me go in for a few minutes' chat. She was on her way to the local Infants' school to fetch Roddy; his school session ended half an hour earlier than the girls, although the Infant and Junior schools were in the same building.

"I go to meet him, then we walk around a bit until the girls come out. That way he can tell me all about what he has been doing; we do have some real nice chats. If you like we can walk down there together."

The children were just coming out of school when we arrived. Roddy caught sight of Ella and came running to meet her. I was amazed at how much he had grown in those few months. As he reached her she stooped to hug him. Released, he looked shyly at me.

"Don't you remember Uncle Ricky?" Ella asked him.

He offered me a hesitant, pudgy hand, but made no effort to kiss me as he used to. I felt a fleeting hurt at this.

"Hello, Roddy," I said.

"Hello."

From the warmth and security of his new world, I was a stranger. One word, and then he turned to Ella and was soon lost in the excitement of recounting the things which, added together, make each day of a child in school a recurrent adventure into discovery.

We strolled around the periphery of the school playground, myself the outsider. "And Mummy . . . ", "and Mummy . . . " Everything breathlessly told as he tried to shape the words he knew into living, breathing pictures. Soon after four o'clock the girls appeared. This time it was different; they were evidently delighted to see me, and chided me on my long absence. I promised to make it up by coming for tea, soon. Promise. Then I said 'goodbye' to them.

Looking back, I saw them going in the opposite direction; Ella and Jackie sedately in step, arms linked; June and Roddy holding hands and skipping along beside them. A family. Each one belonging.

About the Author

E. R. Braithwaite was born in British Guiana (now Guyana) in 1912. Educated at the City College of New York and the University of Cambridge, he served in the Royal Air Force during World War II. Braithwaite spent 1950 to 1960 in London, first as a schoolteacher and then as a welfare worker—experiences he describes in *To Sir, With Love* and *Paid Servant*, respectively. In 1966 he was appointed Guyana's ambassador and permanent representative to the United Nations. He has also held positions at the World Veterans Federation and UNESCO, was a professor of English at New York University's Institute for Afro-American Affairs, and taught creative writing at Howard University. The author of five nonfiction books and two novels, he currently lives in Washington, DC.

EBOOKS BY E. R. BRAITHWAITE

FROM OPEN ROAD MEDIA

Available wherever ebooks are sold

OPEN ROAD

INTEGRATED MEDIA

OPEN ROAD
INTEGRATED MEDIA

Open Road Integrated Media is a digital publisher and multimedia content company. Open Road creates connections between authors and their audiences by marketing its ebooks through a new proprietary online platform, which uses premium video content and social media.

learning experienced not to take
things for granted. Bad timing I
should have been more considerate of Time only 2 yrs post
+ christmas. I invaded I private
Time + space + for so long.
TuG. for showing me this help me
be less intrusive + more considerate. I'm grateful
  TUG for directing me not to
divulge more of my self my life